SWABIA

a culinary tour

Hans-Dieter Reichert
Dieter Wägerle

SWABIA
a culinary tour

With 75 recipes
from south-west Germany
photographed exclusively
for this book
by
Hans Joachim Döbbelin

Translation:
Louise and Desmond Clayton

SIGLOCH
Edition

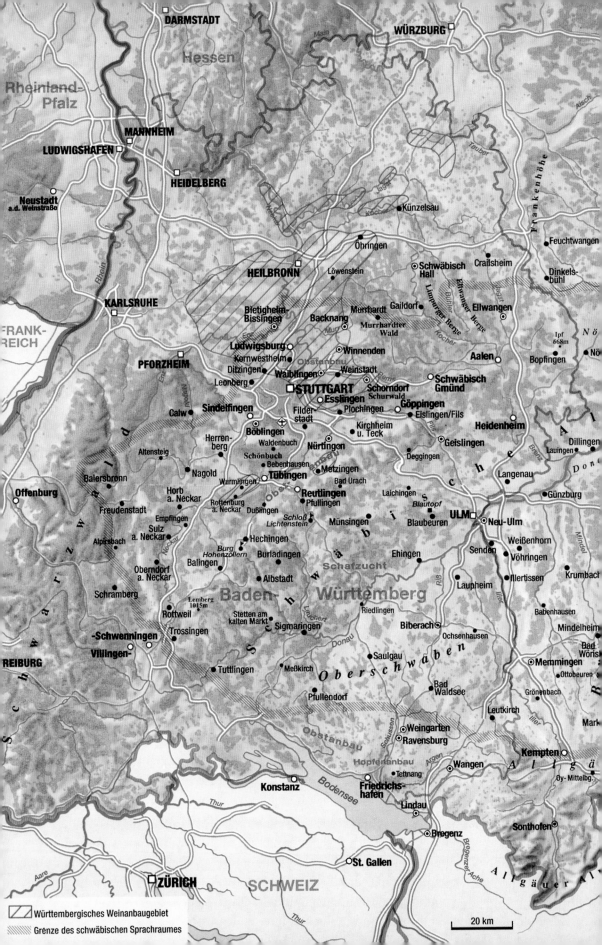

DARMSTADT

WÜRZBURG

Hessen

Rheinland=
Pfalz

MANNHEIM

LUDWIGSHAFEN

HEIDELBERG

Neustadt
a.d. Weinstraße

Künzelsau

FRANK-
REICH

KARLSRUHE

Öhringen

Frankenhöhe

Feuchtwangen

Schwäbisch
Hall

Crailsheim

Dinkels-
bühl

HEILBRONN

Löwenstein

Bietigheim-
Bissingen

Murrhardt

Gaildorf

Ellwangen

PFORZHEIM

Backnang

Murrhardter
Wald

Limpurger Berge

Ellwanger Berge

Ludwigsburg

Winnenden

Aalen

Ipf
668m

Kornwestheim

Obstbau

Weinstadt

Bopfingen

Ditzingen

Waiblingen

Leonberg

STUTTGART

Schorndorf

Schwäbisch
Gmünd

Calw

Sindelfingen

Esslingen

Schurwald

Göppingen

Plochingen

Eislingen/Fils

Filder-
stadt

Heidenheim

Böblingen

Kirchheim
u. Teck

Geislingen

Herren-
berg

Waldenbuch

Nürtingen

Dillingen

Altensteig

Schönbuch

Deggingen

Lauingen

Nagold

Bebenhausen

Metzingen

Langenau

Donau

Baiersbronn

Wurmlingen

Tübingen

Bad Urach

Günzburg

Horb
a. Neckar

Reutlingen

Laichingen

Freudenstadt

Rottenburg
a. Neckar

Pfullingen

Blautopf

Empfingen

Dußlingen

Münsingen

Blaubeuren

ULM

Sulz
a. Neckar

Schloß
Lichtenstein

Neu-Ulm

Alpirsbach

Hechingen

Weißenhorn

Offenburg

Burg
Hohenzollern

Burladingen

Ehingen

Senden

Vöhringen

Oberndorf
a. Neckar

Ballingen

Illertissen

Krumbach

Schramberg

Albstadt

Baden-

Württemberg

Laupheim

Babenhausen

Lemberg
1015m

Riedlingen

Mindelheim

Rottweil

Stetten am
kalten Markt

Sigmaringen

Biberach

Ochsenhausen

Bad
Wörishofen

-Schwenningen

Trossingen

Schafzucht

Saulgau

Oberschwaben

Memmingen

Villingen-

Tuttlingen

Meßkirch

Ottobeuren

REIBURG

Donau

Bad
Waldsee

Grönenbach

Pfullendorf

Mark

Leutkirch

Obstanbau

Weingarten

Konstanz

Bodensee

Ravensburg

Hopfenanbau

Kempten

Allgä

Friedrichs-
hafen

Tettnang

Wangen

Öy- Mittelbg.

Lindau

Sonthofen

ZÜRICH

SCHWEIZ

St. Gallen

Bregenz

Allgäuer Al

CONTENTS

Page 2, and above:
Two of Swabia's highlights:
On its way through the
Swabian Uplands, the
young Danube has created
rocky bastions such as
Stiegelesfels (above). But
rain and river water often
drain off too quickly from
the hard, craggy Jurassic
limestone, leaving the
ground too dry for
farming.
However, where this is not
the case – on the slopes
beneath Wurmlingen
Chapel, for example –
orchards and vineyards
flourish. The chapel's
striking site above the
Neckar Valley has made
it far more than a local
landmark.

Dear Readers,
We do not have to tell you that
Swabian is a world language!
There are, after all, few spots on
this globe where Swabian is not
heard – and not only because of
the Swabian tourists. After all, for
a couple of centuries before the
age of water pipe-lines, tractors,
and other modern agricultural
aids, many Swabians were forced
to leave their homeland for other
parts of the world, because the
arid Swabian Uplands could not
feed them all – a situation
summed up in the saying: "In
Swabia we don't pick at our food,
we eat it!"
But times have changed – the
stodgy, economical dishes of
those days, are a thing of the
past. Swabian inventiveness,
which has given the world cars,
zeppelins, and calculating
machines, for example, has also
flourished in the culinary sphere,
to produce a host of lighter,
tempting variations on traditional
recipes.
Yes, Swabian is a world language,
but perhaps there are a few
readers who are not fluent in it.
They will find a short glossary
of Swabian culinary terms on
page 52.
And with that, we wish you "bon
appetit", or *en guete*, as we say
at home!
Yours
Dieter Wägerle and
Hans-Dieter Reichert

6

Food and Drink Keep Body and Soul Together

This is no doubt true, but on the body alone the effect can be disastrous. As my old uncle, a stout trencherman and wassailer if there ever was one, sometimes points out: "I can watch myself expand. And yet I never eat more than three times a day!" He is past his mid-seventies, and is Swabian. I am also Swabian, and if I want to avoid exceeding the mid-seventies in terms of kilos on my bathroom scales, I have to pull myself together twice a day to keep my growth-orientated body in check. Then the soul rejoices even more when the body is presented with a favourite dish, or the taste-buds are titilated at least once a day with a Swabian delicacy. In short, I love eating, but have to weight-watch rigourously if I am not to end up looking like a walking dumpling. So my days are dominated alternately by desire and vanity, which at times is bound to lead to frustration, or *Luschdverluschd*, as the Swabians put it (in German: *Lustverlust*) meaning deprival of enjoyment. I have to live with this form of frustration. A certain resemblance to the anatomically aesthetic appeal of that Greek discus-thrower has to be paid for in the course of a year by abstaining from at least 730 portions of delicacies with such resounding names as *Knöchla, Haxa, Rippla*, or *Schwartamaga*, the meaning of which will become clear in the course of this book, or, for sweet-tooths, of *Schwarzwälder Kirschtorte*, a variety of cake which most travellers to Germany will have encountered. The Swabian principle "it should be good and not too little" is not calculated to keep the figure in check. When I was drinking coffee in a well-known Stuttgart café one day, a rotund lady chatting to her neighbour at the next table summed the situation up with: "There are no two ways about it, either you eat or you keep your figure. I have decided in favour of my figure!" And having said that, she ordered a plum tart with lashings of cream.

Perhaps she believed in the dictum put forward by Virginia Woolf in "A Room of One's Own": "One cannot think well, love well, sleep well, if one has not dined well", and went home to a good dinner!

How lucky we are that at least in cookery books food is completely harmless if only read about. A colleague of mine has a collection of fifty cookery books, and has

Overleaf:
Lively market-day scenes such as this one in Esslingen are repeated in many places throughout Swabia. And how about taking a little refreshment after shopping – in the "Hirsch" (Stag), "Ochsen" (Ox), or the "Goldenes Lamm" (Golden Lamb), all typical names for Swabian inns?

remained slim. This is due to the fact that he can read but not cook. We can talk together for hours about food. He is a connoisseur, but only in his thoughts. He explores a five-course menu with the same enthusiasm as he does the Sahara, which he has also never done in practice. Once, when we were sitting on my flowery balcony on a fine summer evening, and I served him a Swabian sausage salad, accompanied by a dry Trollinger wine, he came out with: "This is an oasis of rural delights!" He is, admittedly, a poet, who intensifies his enjoyment by all kinds of self-imposed restraints, whether on balconies, in simple inns, or in first-rate restaurants – which he also occasionally patronizes. Both caviar and tripe can delight him. His curiosity is unlimited, and he will get just as much enjoyment out of the quotations in the next column as out of a mental journey through the cuisine of Canton.

Recent years have seen a tendency to Frenchify menus, and the dog-Latin one is presented with in some of the more fashionable restaurants tends to get on my nerves and ruin my appetite. It is, of course, a fine thing that the

Every man should eat and drink, and enjoy the good of all his labour, it is the gift of God.
(Ecclesiastes 3:13)

I hate a man who swallows, affecting not to know what he is eating.
I suspect his taste in higher matters.
(Charles Lamb. Essays of Elia)

A man is in general better pleased when he has a good dinner upon his table, than when his wife talks Greek.
(Samuel Johnson. Quoted in Birbeck Hill's Johnsonian Miscellanies)

The discovery of a new dish does more for the happiness of mankind than the discovery of a star.
(Anthelme Brillat-Savarin. Physiologie de goût)

Bad cooks – and the utter lack of reason in the kitchen – have delayed human development longest and impaired it most.
(F. W. Nietzsche. Jenseits von Gut und Böse)

The broom hung outside an inn indicates that "Federweisser" (new, only partly fermented, wine) is being served. The experienced Federweisser drinker goes to the inn on foot – he knows why!

variety of cuisines available in the big towns has expanded tremendously in the last few decades: to the ubiquitous Chinese restaurants have been added Japanese, Vietnamese, Thai, and Korean, for example, not all of them good, of course, and there has been an "invasion" of cooks or would-be cooks from many parts of Europe. In some areas this has gone so far that, although practically every village has its Pizzaria Roma, or its Chinese Mandarin, it is hard to find a restaurant serving local food. And that is where I draw the line. In general I like to keep both feet on my home ground, as it were, to orientate myself on the Swabian cuisine, to talk Swabian, eat Swabian, drink Swabian, and pay Swabian (which means not overpay, but should not be taken to mean being niggardly with tips!).

And now: do food and drink keep body and soul together? Of course they do! And no matter how one controls one's girth – by moderation or judicious use of a belt – food and drink are two of the three so often cited "best things in life". Goethe, that great bon viveur, was convinced of this. His praise of Swabia is rapturous: "Let us escape to Swabia! Help, oh heaven! You will find sweet dishes there, and all good things in abundance . . . And in Swabia the bread is baked with butter and eggs."

These words are spoken by Reynard the Fox in Goethe's epic "Reineke der Fuchs" in an effort to persuade his wife to flee with him from the king to the Promised Land, and apparently all he could think of was sweet dishes and bread. The poet, who certainly knew his stuff when it came to eating and drinking well, was surely a trifle excessive there. But he speaks very favourably of the Swabian cuisine, wines, and countryside, elsewhere, too; and on his travels he certainly tried a number of more tempting delicacies than just sweet dishes, bread, *Spätzle* and *Knöpfle* – after all, our ancestors did not only live on milk, flour, sugar, and eggs: there were also vegetables, fruit, meat, poultry, game, and fish, not to mention the wine, which the Romans had introduced. In fact, however, the main drinks in those days were beer and cider, for simple people, apart from the wine-growers themselves, could not normally afford to drink wine. The modern prayer: "Give us this day our

daily Trollinger", only came into fashion after the second world war.

It must be said, however, that few Swabians have gourmet ambitions, for they are not really in keeping with the fundamental, rural simplicity of our cuisine. And yet we do know what is good, and there is an increasing interest in refined enjoyment of food and drink. The influence of our pietistic ancestors, mainly in the Württemberg region, is gradually being replaced by more sophisticated tastes, also among young people. Fast food is going out, and ketchup is something for the kids. Good food is becoming increasingly international. Competition is increasing – and my friend Ernesto from Bari likes to eat in a Swabian restaurant on his day off. If that is not a sign of the times, what is?

There is a good reason why Swabian wines – unlike cars from Swabia – are hardly known outside the region: Swabian wine-lovers prefer to drink the Trollingers, Silvaners, Rieslings, and other wines from vineyards like this one on Rotenberg near Stuttgart, themselves.

WELL BAKED . . .

For the priest in Berg near Ravensburg, who is celebrating the Palm Sunday service, the pretzel, with its intertwined arms, symbolizes eternity.

Bacha, baked, is a word used in a number of important variations in Swabian. To be *nicht recht bacha* (not well-baked) is the equivalent of being "half-baked" in English. *Altbacha*, which, in reference to bread, means a few days old, no longer fresh, and is figuratively used to mean old-fashioned, is, on the other hand, often said proudly by people of themselves to imply slightly conservative, behind the times, and, by further implication, not given to present-day vices. *Obacha*, meaning unbaked, not purified by the heat of the oven, or, if you like, by purgatory, stands for unmodern, impossible, ill-mannered, unfinished, brainless, and immoderate. To ask a politician to tell the truth, for example, would be *obacha*. *Rechtbacha*, well-baked, means above criticism, everything that a good loaf, bread roll, or biscuit ought to be, so that it does not lie heavy on the stomach or cause biliousness. It is up to the *Beck*, the baker, to produce well-baked bread, or he will risk being classed as a *Beckaseggl* a term of abuse for a lazy person, which can equally well be applied to butchers, journalists, professors, or politicians, if they are lacking in mental energy, creativity, or imagination. In view of this, Swabian bakers should be pleased that they, or their trade, are used as a standard by which others can also be judged. On the other hand, the baker often used to be regarded quite unfairly as lazy, but rightly as easy-going. Butchers jokingly said that to pass the "baker's exam" you had to be able to stare out of a window for an hour without thinking. The fact that bakers have always had to start their work in the small hours of the morning is often forgotten – so why should they not, between batches, hang out of the window for a while to get a breath of fresher, cooler air, and pass their "exam" at the same time? I could go on kneading this dough – warming up half-baked loaves – for some time . . .
There are a number of baker's specialities for which we Swabians like to believe we have gained worldwide renown. There is, for example, the story about the baker from Urach, who had committed some crime and was going to be hanged for it unless – as pronounced by the feudal lord sitting in judgement – he succeeded in baking a loaf through which the light of the sun would fall three times. His canny wife,

who was present when judgement was passed, folded her arms; the miscreant understood the sign, and saved his life by baking the world's first pretzel. Similar stories are of course told elsewhere to illustrate the inventiveness of bakers of other regions. So let us regard it simply as a compliment to all clever baker's wives, and their expressive arms. For one thing is sure: the arms are the most important thing about a pretzel, and in view if this we must assume that the legendary inventor of the Bavarian pretzel had considerably more powerful upper limbs than her Swabian cousin, otherwise the difference between the two forms of pretzel would hardly have persisted to this day. But of course they are not all the same in Swabia, either, thank goodness – if they were, the Swabians would lose one of their best-loved debating points! After all, there are not a few people who are prepared to go for miles for the best pretzels in the area. And if you should send an expatriate Swabian girl a pretzel as a reminder of her homeland, it will be received – no matter whether it has become

A Swabian could hardly imagine a baker who does not offer fresh pretzels every day.

Stuttgart, the capital of Baden-Württemberg, the "city set among woods and vineyards". Most Stuttgarters still prefer to think of their town in such terms rather than as "partner of the world", as a more recent slogan dubs it.

stone-hard or completely limp in transit – with home-sick tears of delight, and if necessary will be dunked in the cup of tea or the café au lait to make it biteable. By serving simply a glass of red wine and a pretzel at many receptions given for high-ranking international guests, Stuttgart's economical Lord Mayor, Manfred Rommel, has made it clear that the simple pleasures of life can often be the best. It must be admitted that the fellow is usually *recht bacha*, although he does occasionally tend to beat about the bush for a time, and may even end by capping his speech with a half-baked joke.

The basis for good bread is, of course, good flour. And here Swabia and the German-speaking countries in general are very particular about quality – and produce a wide variety of types which is reflected in the wide variety of breads available even in small village bakeries. The choice is far greater than the "brown" or "white" loaf alternatives offered in many other parts of the world. Here, wheat does not have the allpowerful position it occupies elsewhere – rye flour is almost equally important, and various other grains are now also used,

mixed in varying proportions to produce breads ranging from pure white to almost black. In recent years the "baguette" has become popular – but here it must be admitted that the French do it better!

The German word *Seelen* normally means "souls", but when we Swabians refer to *Seelen* we generally mean long, flat white loaves, crisp on the outside, and soft with many holes inside. They, too, vary greatly in type and quality. They come sprinkled with salt and caraway seeds, or with sugar or poppy seeds, and can be made of lighter or darker flour. Visitors often recall with enthusiasm their first encounter with these delights, or with our onion tarts – both provide a worth-while glimpse of the Swabian way of doing things and the Swabian art of baking – and insist that they have never again found any that came up to the very first ones they tried.

The inbuilt resistance of our northern neighbours to non-sweet pastries seems to melt away under southern skies, where, from what one hears, there is even something called *Pizza di cipolle*. The phrase "from what one hears", is only too appropri-

ate in this context, of course, and the Swabian onion tart, too, naturally not only tickles the palate but also the nose and ear: it is not nicknamed "trumpet tart" for nothing! Heinz-Eugen Schramm has written a dialect poem on this phenomenon in which he maintains that passing wind is a healthy act. The fact that he is not alone in this opinion was revealed in no uncertain terms on one occasion, when I was in a pub where "new wine" was on sale, which is traditionally accompanied by onion tart. A man sitting at a neighbouring table, a local plumber or carpenter, perhaps, having enjoyed two pieces of "trumpet tart" relieved his flatulence in no uncertain way. His only comment was: "What I lack in manners I gain in health!" His friend smiled at me, and excused the noisy demonstration with the words: "He's never been one for farting about!"

Fortunately, Swabia, like most other German-speaking areas has largely preserved its baking traditions. Here, small bakeries still predominate, so that most people have a wide choice of bakers to choose from. Smallish places with only a couple of thousand inhabi-

tants will often boast two or three bakers. This is in strong contrast to British and American communities, where large industrial bakers often have a near-monopoly. The trend in Swabia nowadays is to try out new things – combining them if possible with traditional ones. And so here and there old disused village bakehouses are even being put back into commission – which means that in addition to their basic function they also once again serve as centres for social interaction, in other words, the ladies of the village, young and old, meet there for a good gossip. Recipes are exchanged, and otherwise conservative Swabian housewives find themselves taking an interest in foreign specialities: a piece of onion tart will be exchanged for a slice of pizza or a wedge of flat Turkish bread. The village bakehouse as an international forum – and everything homemade, loaf for loaf.

In view of such intense and open-minded interest in baked goods of all kinds, it is not surprising that the Swabians can boast of having the world's oldest bread museum. In 1955 Dr W. Eisele founded the German Bread Museum in Ulm, using his own

large collection as a basis, and since then people from far and near come day in and day out to look at this fascinating record of the world's bread and its history. Coverage is comprehensive, beginning with the practical side of grain production, and proceeding from there to milling and baking techniques: old baking tins and forms, bread stamps, and modern bakery equipment. But there are also exhibits from the fields of art and culture: pictures, coins and medals, posters, placques, and seals reveal the importance that bread has had for mankind at all ages and on all continents – and ration coupons recall periods of shortage during times of war and need. Such an extensive theme cannot be depicted adequately here, but an illustration overleaf of one of the Ulm exhibits proves a visual introduction to our next, closely related theme.

Not only bread, but also fruit or onion tart benefit from being baked in a wood-fired oven. Perhaps there still are some village bakers who bake their customers' home-made cakes and loaves for them.

DOUGHS, BATTERS, PASTRIES . . .

Oscar Wilde – unfortunately not a Swabian – is immortalized in Swabian dialect in the phrase "Nach'ma guata Essa kosch jedem vergebba, sogar dr oigena Verwandschaft", which translates back into English as "After dining well one can forgive anybody, even one's own relations."
And yet I venture to doubt whether Oscar Wilde would willingly have dined on "Brota, Spätzla ond gmischtem Salat" – roast meat, Swabian pasta, and mixed salad. To non-Swabians it is indeed a rather surprising combination, and one not exactly conducive to the lissom figure, although it becomes quite clear when one has seen enough Swabian housewives that lissom is a word that does not carry much weight, as it were, in their kitchens. When it comes to cooking, and food in general they, and their "better halves" believe in plenty of everything, and it is not surprising to learn that the number of heavyweights in Swabia is well above the national average. "We eat the way we work – heartily", is a local saying. In the country, Swabian weddings, baptisms, and confirmations are often a welcome excuse for several days of feasting on the solid dishes so typical of the local cuisine – days which are bitterly paid for in subsequent days of fasting, or, if this price is too high, with an inch or two more round the waist. But girth is nothing to be ashamed of in this region, on the contrary, it has been dearly bought! When two fat people marry, a typical comment might be: "That'll be a full double bed!" The lean, sporty figure is accepted as an ideal, but the philosophy of every-day life recognizes it as no more than an approximate, utopian value, and the truly modest person is honest enough to admit the hopelessness of combining it with the pleasures of the flesh plus the appropriate side-dishes. And to be honest: it is impossible to get – or provide – a real grip on life without a certain pound-age. That applies to both sexes. A chap who has "no backside in his pants" is unlikely to have much else to offer. And a woman who is as flat as a board or as thin as a rake cannot have a heart, because there is no room for it behind her non-existent bosom. Heine once wrote: "Her bosom was as flat as Lüneburg Heath." She could hardly have been a Swabian! However, there is an infinite

number of variations between a twiggy and a Rubens figure – with an equal number of charms. "Variety is the very spice of life, that gives it all its flavour", as William Cowper put it. I am far from suggesting that the full Swabian figure suits everybody. The well-balanced compromise can perhaps be found somewhere in the middle, and flabby flesh is clearly not attractive: good meat is marbled and firm. A gourmet once described the anatomy of his mistress to me as: "*al dente*, the way *Spätzle* and spaghetti should be". Soft, yet providing a certain resistance to the bite, as one might say – also with regard to the psyche.

This sensual digression says much about the quality of a cuisine. A cuisine is only as good as the people that create it and live with it. To quote Heinrich Heine once again:

"Every country has its characteristic cuisine and its characteristic women, and in such things everything is a matter of taste. One person likes roast chicken, another roast duck. For myself, I love roast chicken, roast duck, and roast goose. Are British beauties not just as healthy, nourishing, solid, consistent, artless, and yet

Bread, cakes, "Spätzle" – without flour they could not be made. The Ulm Bread Museum contains, in addition to the 18th century printing block for sacks, shown on the left, a great number of exhibits related to milling and baking; and in the mill at Dauchingen on the upper Neckar, shown above, we see how flour is still ground in the old, traditional way.

19

as excellent, as Old England's simple, good food?

There we find no smiling fricassée, no flighty vol-au-vent, no sighing, intellectual ragoût, none of those thousand-fold variations of stuffed, braised, roasted, sugared, piquant, pretentious, declamatory and sentimental dishes of the kind we find in a French restaurant and which have a lot in common with the lovely French women themselves!"

A Swabian version of this would have to aim at a healthy compromise, which might run something like: Swabian women are as substantial as a good loaf, as light and sweet as Carnival cakes, as sound as well-made *Spätzle*, as intricate as a pretzel, as radiant as fresh *Flädle*, as light as yeast dumplings, as seductive as warm plum tart, as economical as a semolina soup, as stunning as an onion tart.

In keeping with the theme of this chapter, the above selection of comparisons is based on products using flour. If I wanted to characterize Swabian femininity by seeking comparisons throughout the entire cuisine, then a thousand further facets would have to be added.

Well, how about it – shall we make *Spätzle*, or shall we eat the dough as it is? – this purely rhetorical question is answered many thousand times a day in Swabian households with: sure, we'll make them! We (the two authors) make them by hand, mark you, although *Spätzle* machines have long since been accepted by the cack-handed and the lazy.

For Christians, the Forbidden Fruit was the apple, for Mohammedans, however, it was the banyan or fig. One wonders whether, had Adam and Eve been Swabians, the Garden of Eden might not have sported a *Spätzle* tree as the ultimate temptation. If that had been the case, there is no doubt that even a Swabian Adam and Eve would have succumbed, because: how easily *Spätzle* find their way to the inner man! I dare say that the popularity of the Italians living in our region is at least partly based on the fact that their cuisine also contains many pasta dishes. The relationship between various forms of flour-paste is obvious. On the basis of flour-paste, co-existence is merely a matter of time, for the individual forms of preparation are simply a matter of form. We have long since called

maccaroni "tunnel *Spätzle*" – tunnel noodles. And, of course, wine is another interest shared by Swabians and Italians – but that is another story.

In the dish called *Gaisburger Marsch* – a kind of stew – potatoes and *Spätzle* celebrate a tasty wedding. Quite a few people from the north of Germany are tempted by the potato bait in this dish, try it, and go on from there to explore Swabian cookery. The result is inevitable: they get hooked on the joys of the Swabian cuisine, and themselves become some of its strongest champions. There is one dialect term that I find unacceptable: "lazy-woman's *Spätzle*", meaning flat noodles, for no matter how important one might think home-made ingredients are, it should not be forgotten that the swaggering, chauvinistic, self-appointed gourmet cooks who use such phrases are precisely the ones who tend to treat their wives as kitchen skivvies.

The authors cooperate at making "Spätzle": Wägerle tries to stay out of hot water while Reichert lands the catch.

More than just Cabbage and Beet

Many eulogies have been written on the potato and on sauerkraut. But who has written a song of praise to the conical white cabbage that thrives particularly in the Filder area to the south of Stuttgart, and that makes the best sauerkraut? The Filder area naturally also produces the ordinary white cabbage and the red cabbage, as the picture on the right makes clear.

It is not so long ago that the German saying "What the peasant doesn't know he won't eat", was still regarded as a valid way of describing the narrow horizon of the rustic. In the meantime the peasant has become a farmer, familiar with exotic products from abroad and ready to try to grow them in his fields. The farmer now has to think in terms of very narrow profit-margins, and so cabbage, beet and other root vegetables, milk and meat, have to be supplemented with all kinds of additional products which go with the countryside, soil, and climate. The basis is still the soil, and the aim is to get the best economic use out of it without over-exploiting it and without damaging it by the use of too much chemistry. Two of the new virtues expected of our farmers are ecological responsibility and imagination. Ideally, the farmer is at the same time producer and conservationist. When I speak of farmers, I also mean our fruit and vegetable farmers, and, of course, the wine-growers, all of whom contribute equally to the variety to be found in our kitchens and cellars. Variety is very much in demand, but without the cabbage and root vegetables even the

Spätzle-Swabian would feel deprived. Potato salad alone would be enough to qualify the potato as a basic foodstuff, while potato soup, fried potatoes, mashed potato, potato cake, potato soufflé, and various specifically Swabian forms of using potatoes, which will be found among the recipes, must be classed as true delicacies. We have already referred to the marriage of the *Spätzle* and the potato in the dish called Gaisburg Stew. And we should not forget "Sour Potato wheels", which economical housewives used to make out of left-over potato salad; today the danger of salmonella poisoning is in everyone's mind, and so we prefer to use freshly-boiled potatoes for this dish. We Swabians also combine flour and potato when we serve pancakes with potato salad. But there is one potato dish that I will never consent to eat: chips with ketch-up. Otherwise I find potatoes acceptable in any form: baked, steamed, boiled, stuffed, fried, sliced, grated, or mashed, in soups, fritters, or nests. If only they did not have to be peeled! In view of all this, we cannot have anything against the Prussians for being "potato-lovers", nor against Sir Francis Drake for

having brought the potato from America to Europe in the 16th century, after which it was soon introduced to a number of European countries. By 1619 it was sufficiently established in England to be served at the Royal table – but it was not an immediate success everywhere. In many places it was at first regarded as poisonous and in 1630, for example, the Diet of Besançon forbade its cultivation for fear of leprosy. Once established, however, it became one of the staple foods throughout Europe, and people even enthused about the potato flower, which became a popular decorative motif for crockery.

But now it is time to pay suitable homage to the cabbage. Cabbage belongs to the extensive cruciferous family which includes the mini edition called Brussels sprouts. The Swabian cuisine uses red and white cabbage – the latter both round and conical –, savoy cabbage, green cabbage, and cauliflower. There is also kohlrabi; and broccoli, too, has now entered the Swabian kitchen. Researchers maintain that cabbage already formed part of the Celtic cuisine: so our pre-Swabian-Alammanic forebears were already

He who distinguishes the true savor of his food can never be a glutton; he who does not cannot be otherwise.
(H.D. Thoreau. Higher Laws)

krauts! The best in the cabbage line is the conical white cabbage from the high plateau, called *Filder*, to the south of Stuttgart. This type is also called *Filder-kraut* in German after the area in which it is principally grown; it is a delicacy in a different class to the normal round white cabbage, but now the round ones are more common than the conical form even in the Filder area, because they can be more easily processed in the sauerkraut factories. Most *Filderkraut* is produced by about ninety farmers organized in cooperatives which also market the produce for about 10,000 marks gross per hectare – not exactly princely pay, but at least regular. Properly prepared and served, sauerkraut really is something special, and the tradition in Germany goes back a long way. The poet Ludwig Uhland (1787–1862) might well have eaten sauerkraut at the inn called "Hirsch" (The Stag) in Echterdingen in the Filder region, for it is known that he dined there a number of times, as did quite a few other distinguished people, including Lavater, Schiller, Goethe, Hegel, Hauff, Mörike, Lenau, Kerner, and Gerok; and it is also known that Count Zeppelin

was a *Filderkraut* fan.
One of Ludwig Uhland's poems includes a few lines which translate very roughly as follows:

And our noble sauerkraut,
of that there is no doubt,
was first invented by a German
to serve at dinner or at luncheon.
When garnished with some tender meat,
the whole arranged so mild and neat,
the effect's like Venus bedded amongst the roses.

Left page: Nestled in a valley in the wooded Schönbuch Hills near Tübingen, is the former monastery of Bebenhausen, crowned by the ornate ridge turret of its church. After sight-seeing duties are over, the visitor can enjoy a traditional Swabian snack in one of the village's inns – or an opulent meal.

BENEATH A TREE SO GREEN AND MILD

He who would have the fruit must climb the tree. (Thomas Fuller. Gnomologia)

Right: Who has the finest sheep? Here they are, grazing under blossoming fruit trees near Dürrwangen in the Swabian Uplands.

Ludwig Uhland wrote a poem beginning with the above words, in which he describes the pleasures of lying beneath an apple tree, and looking up into its branches; he compares it to an inn where the best of food and drink is to be found, and the softest bed, and where the guests sing happily all day long. It is a description of one of life's delights which is still available and which everyone can afford. All we need is time and a little understanding for our green "host". We really do not have to start thinking in practical terms of preserving, or of apple tart with cream, of apple fritters, apple juice, cider . . . Just appreciating nature, forgetting the stomach for a while, and letting one's thoughts roam the skies, also enhances the quality of life. And, believe me, such breaks are necessary. Little dreams enhance reality. We really do not straightaway have to start spraying the tree with insecticide!

Real Swabian housewives and "househusbands" also subconsciously appreciate the poetry of a pretty garden or orchard, but their consciousness is nevertheless full of practical considerations. For true Swabians, a ripe red cherry or raspberry will only rarely conjure up pictures of expectantly open cherry-like lips – they will think of jam, or syrup, or raspberry brandy. It is with such things in mind that the Swabian will tend a garden or orchard, harvest fruit, and make preserves, with jam leading the way. Jam-making is regarded as an artform in Swabia; the factory-made article from the shelves of the supermarket is despised. Home-made jam is prepared to thousands of different recipes, and the result is always unique; vintage, playing the same part as it does with wine, and all kinds of subtle psychic vibes emanating from the cook, are incorporated in the product. Home-made jam is not simply something to spread on your bread: like home-made brandy, it is a philosophy. If you want to pay a compliment to a jam-maker, you have to blatantly ask to try a little. With luck you will then be presented with enough samples to cover a large part of your jam needs, and will moreover be accepted as a connoisseur.

The Swabian word for jam – *Gsälz* – is connected with the history of preserving food. Salt was still the most common preserving agent even in the last

Ripe apples from Swabia – there is a wide variety for every taste: the choice is yours!

century, although it was not used for berries or other fruit. Fruit could at the most be turned into cider, wine, or brandy, or dried, because imported cane sugar was too expensive for most people. The sweet pleasures of jam making only arrived with the advent of beet sugar. Salt, in its capacity as a preserving agent, then lent its name to sugar in this process. Since then we have been able to enjoy black and red currant jam, strawberry, gooseberry, raspberry, and blackberry jam – and cherry, plum, apricot, peach, and quince are, of course, also excellent for jam making. And they can be mixed for the purpose to make three or four-fruit jam. But only part of the brilliant golden, red, or blue blessings from our orchards or gardens ends up in the form of jams or preserved fruit, as juice or cider, or in the deep-freeze. Another part is reserved for higher things. In baskets, crates, or tall casks, it is taken to the distilleries to be found in the villages or suburbs. Refined, and "spiritualized", after a year or so spent in the darkness of a cellar, the resulting clear water of life offers pleasure, relaxation, and even relief after a heavy meal. Many English people –

and Americans, perhaps, too – confuse fruit brandy with liqueur. They expect it to be sweet, so that those who are looking forward to something sweet when they order it are horrified at its dryness, and those who like a dry spirit without the addition of syrup do not even try it. Others again play safe by ordering a cognac, and never discover how good a spirit distilled from apples, pears, or from a mixture of fruits (then called *Obstler*) can be. But whether it be a noble spirit, or a simple, well-made fruit brandy, take my advice: drink in moderation, for as John Lyly said: "Long quaffing maketh a short life".

The Swabians are very fond of fruit in every form, whether raw, stewed, as jam, juice, or brandy. No one has ever listed all the distilleries in Swabia, but there are about 24,000 in the south-west corner of Germany where Swabia lies – 78 per cent of all the German distilleries!

A Bit of Meat won't do us any Harm!

A 13th century song in praise of food runs: "Geese and capons, birds, and swine, sausage and peacocks: on them we'll dine!" In the Middle Ages the well-to-do were certainly not modest in their eating habits. There are many songs referring to the medieval tendency to overdo things at table. There were tracts enough on table manners, too. "Some are such gormandizers that they do not watch their mouths, and bite their own hands in their haste: no courtly gentleman should behave so greedily!" What does this tell us? – That the knightly folk, the lords – and possibly even the ladies – voraciously devoured the best things available at the time.

The middle classes, once they were established, also did themselves proud at table: one only has to think of the descriptions given by Samuel Pepys of how he wined and dined his guests in the 18th century; and high-ranking officials throughout Europe rarely had to go hungry. The bill of fare for a nuptial dinner of a counting house official in France dating from 1571 consisted of only three courses, but the first course comprised no less than fourteen dishes, including salad, soups, roast mutton and roast roebuck, the third course seventeen dishes, mainly tarts and fruits, and the second no less than twenty-one: venison broth, roast capon, orange salad, roast pheasants, roast rabbits, roast spring chickens, some stuffed, some larded, roast crousets, cheriots, and crousets pâtés (whatever they may be), roast quails, smoked tongues, Boulogne sausages, pheasant pâtés, pâté of Meaux ham, turkey or peacock pâté, venison pâté, leg of lamb, capon in aspic, roast swan, sweetened mustard, olives.

However, until our own times, people who could afford such luxury formed a very small section of the European population. The majority of people as likely as not lived on the verge of starvation throughout most of mankind's history.

The menu given above was, of course, for an exceptional occasion, but it tells us what meats were available at that time: beef, pork, mutton, game, and poultry. Oddly enough, it included no fish.

Preserving by smoking and pickling was already known, but storing fresh meat presented considerable difficulties, so that especially "the lower levels of

society" rarely saw meat on their tables in summer – a fact they often complained of, or tried to remedy by insisting on the rights of payment in kind often written into their labour contracts. Game was reserved entirely for the land-owners, the only people licensed to hunt or shoot. Nowadays we take the availability of good meat for granted, and easily forget that in the past – even in our bounti-ful 20th century – a good dish of meat was rarely something to be treated as a matter of course. The neat little houses in some of the outlying parts of Stuttgart no longer betray the history of their origins in the early 1930's. Originally, in addition to a large garden for growing fruit and vegetables, each house was pro-vided with a room for keeping domestic animals. The idea was that the families, most of them large, with an unemployed father, who built the houses themselves, should, in addition to fresh eggs and goat's milk, also occasionally be able to enjoy a dish of meat. Rabbits were kept, fed on fresh dandelion leaves or old lettuce or cabbage leaves, and here and there the grunting of a pig could be heard as it waited for the kitchen waste from the whole

The work to be done at dawn on slaughtering day looks like a mysterious, frightening ritual. After being killed, the pig is scalded with boiling water, and scraped free of bristles. The main work should be done before the day warms up, and the meat made into sausages, or stored away fresh in the deep freeze.

Passers-by seeing the statue of the great poet on Stuttgart's Schiller Square would hardly guess that one of his favourite meals was "Knackwurst" (a kind of Frankfurter) with potatoes. Nowadays the Swabians have a number of favourite dishes – for example, sour kidneys with fried potatoes.

neighbourhood – and there was always someone in the area capable of giving the coup de grâce to a tired old hen destined for the pot.

Today, traces of such semi-rural existences on the fringes of a city are hard to find. But right out in the heart of Swabia, real picture-book farming is still to be found, despite the much-criticized agro-industry. In such places the "family pig" which has been raised from suckling status, will still have a name. But, of course, it will one day also meet its fate: in the early morning it will be killed by the local butcher – in the space between the sty and the house, perhaps, as in the old days – and afterwards will be scalded, cleaned, and cut up. Apart from the tools of his trade, the butcher will also have all the necessary herbs and spices with him for the fresh liver-sausage and black pudding; the housewife herself will have prepared a dish full of chopped onion for the same purpose. There is a lot of work to be done before the meat has been stored away in fridge or deep-freeze. It is communal work, done by the whole family, often with the help of neigh-bours, and there is a lot of gossip-

ing and joking. A party atmos-phere develops, and the day cul-minates in a meal consisting of what is modestly called *Metzel-suppe*, or broth, which is any-thing but what is normally under-stood by the word broth, as it contains various cuts of pork ranging from flank, to heart, and cheek, plus some of the freshly-made liver-sausages and black puddings, sauerkraut, and *Spätzle*. The glass of fruit brandy to round off the meal is a must. When the party breaks up, the guests are given bits and pieces to take home with them – and then comes the inevitable question: "When'll you be slaughtering?" For one thing is sure: if you come to me for sausage-making, I'll come to you in return. In the days when ways of preserving meat were still limited to smoking and various forms of pickling, larger amounts of the fresh meat were probably eaten very soon after slaughtering. In the two-hundred-year-old cookery book by Friederike Luise Löffler, we read under the heading "Fresh roast sirloin on the spit":

"Take either the whole or the half sirloin, as necessary, beat it well, remove the thicker skin, lard as you would a hare, marinate

it in boiling vinegar for an hour, longer if time allows, then rub it all over with pepper, cloves, and salt, and put in on the spit, securing it well with string. Pour the vinegar in which the meat was marinated into a baking pan, add some meat stock, a bay leaf, an onion, and some slices of lemon; baste the roast frequently first with butter, then with its own juices, and roast very slowly. In the mean-time the sauce is prepared as follows: take a tablespoon of finely-chopped shallots, and 60 g of finely chopped anchovies, brown a heaped tablespoon of flour in a little butter, fry the shallots and anchovies in it, pour some of the gravy from the roast and a ladle of broth into it, and add a number of lemon slices, a bay leaf, and a tablespoon of capers. When the roast is ready, the sauce can be poured over it, or served separately."

With her book, "F. L. Löflerin", as the writer called herself at the end of the introduction, created at the end of the 18th century what Hermine Kiehnle achieved in the 20th: a general cookery book which does not deny its Swabian origins and nevertheless achieved wide acceptance. It went through innumerable

Friedrich looks down with pleasure at the wine festival on the square named after him. Perhaps some of the revellers are drinking a "Schiller" – a rosé wine made of red and white grapes planted in mixed lots in the vineyards of the Bottwar and Schozach valleys.

The life of a shepherd in the Swabian Uplands, as here on Witthoh Hill in the west, is far from idyllic. In the course of the year shepherds have to travel long distances with their flocks. The juniper heath-land – like that shown above, on Raichberg near Albstadt-Onstmettingen – formed over the centuries by grazing sheep, has been gradually reduced to a few protected areas by the advance of agro-industrial technology.

editions – by 1930 the original publisher had brought it out no less than 130 times.

Generations of domestic cooks far beyond the bounds of Württemberg have looked up how to prepare "salt beef", or "sauerkraut with stuffed pike", "boudin (pudding) of snipe", or "oyster sauce with poultry and roast veal", or "plain aniseed biscuits" and "a variant with almonds".

After reading such things, one is of course again tempted to speak of the good old days, but they were by no means as good as all that, and certainly not for the majority. I prefer to keep the ground under my feet, and plead for pig's trotters. Although many people have turned their back on pork – admittedly often for good reason – I am still a fan of the meat of the pig.

Another lover of simple pleasures was our "model Swabian" Friedrich Schiller – and in this respect at least I am vain enough to put myself in the same class as him. *Knackwurst* (a kind of Frankfurter) with potatoes was among his, though not my, favourite dishes. And when he returned to Weimar after visiting his native Swabia he usually had a number of smoked sausages in his luggage, made by his sister Louise after the family pig had been slaughtered.

Of course, homemade sausages are now the great exception. In Swabia, too, the honourable trade of butcher is flourishing. The butchers' shops display all kinds of local and foreign temptations – to which we cannot help succumbing on occasion – ranging from liver sausage to mortadella. For anyone who would like to study the history of this trade, it should be pointed out with true Swabian modesty that we also have a special museum devoted to this subject: the *Deutsches Fleischereimuseum* in Böblingen, diagonally across from the Town Hall. If, after satisfying your appetite for pictures, carved chests, silver goblets, and embroidered guild flags, you feel that your inner man must also have his reward, then in one of the butcher's shops in the area you will certainly find a tasty snack in the form of a roll with a slice of hot Swabian meat loaf.

When it is a question of a good roast, a chat with one of our Swabian sheep-farmers can never do any harm. The "good shepherd" still exists, and not only in the Swabian Uplands, even

The prickly carline thistle (Carlina acaulis) is the emblem of the Swabian Uplands. The inhabitants of the "rough hills" are only prickly nowadays when provoked by silly townees.

If the clever donkey agrees with the sheep he only has to cry "y-eah, y-eah!"

though he best fits into that particular kind of countryside. After all, the juniper heath, the characteristic landscape of that region, was formed over the centuries by grazing sheep. The tender shoots of deciduous treses are consumed by the sheep before they can grow, while the prickly, bitter shoots of the juniper resist such attacks, and develop into upright, dark-green bushes which grow in picturesque groups dotted about the hilly countryside. Thanks to similar defensive mechanisms, the carline thistle has also survived – to become the emblem of the Swabian Uplands.

Migrating flocks of sheep are now regarded as agents of conservation. Shepherding is an idyllic-seeming occupation, but is commercially scarcely viable, and only the devoted few keep it up. They stay with their flocks – and, with their traditional annual shepherds' races, have even succeeded in becoming a tourist attraction. But foreign producers are increasingly invading the market, and shepherding is no longer just a hard day-and-night rearing and shearing job, but also a tough margin-clipping business.

My "good shepherd" lives in the eastern part of the Uplands, if he is not in the process of driving his sheep through the countryside, a trek covering a couple of hundred kilometres, constantly under threat from lethal cars and motorbikes, aggressive land developers and stubborn local councillors. Werner Wiedenmann is a dedicated shepherd. In 1962 he took over the sheep-farm from his then eighty-four-year-old mother. He has always been, and will always remain, a shepherd. Fate has granted him a son who is not afraid of the hard work involved, and his wife faithfully mans the office at home. The family business succeeds because it is run on such harmonious lines. The shepherd grows his winter fodder on his own 28 hectares of land, and the sixteen or eighteen hour day for both man and dogs has never been regarded as a dog's life by the shepherd or his family. The fourth generation is already at work, and the Master of Animal Husbandry, as Werner Wiedenmann is entitled to call himself, continues to stick to his trade. By selling direct to the consumer he can just about survive in this competitive age, but only because the whole family cooperates.

"Eight hundred lambs", he says, "are a good year, and you can live

The traditional Shepherds' Races in Urach (top picture), Heidenheim, and Markgröningen should really be renamed "Female Animal Keeper's Races", because that is now the official German title of a shepherdess – to which only a stupid donkey could cry "y-eah, y-yeah"!

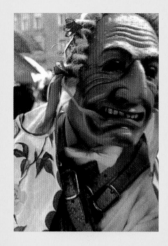

Swabian Carnevalists in action.

Double page overleaf: Looking across the bare top of Burren Hill (on the right-hand side of the picture) near Geisslingen an der Steige we can see the trough that runs across the Uplands and provides ideal walking country. The Swabian Hikers' Association alone has 120,000 members.

on them. But that's enough, and that's the way it'll stay."
Leaving the realities of country life, and returning to the kitchen and dining table, we stumble across the saying "Hidden meat is also meat", which at first seems to make little sense. But it refers to the possibility of eating meat in a form that conceals it, and specifically to the Swabian speciality called *Maultaschen*, which has heretically been described as a kind of giant ravioli, and in which the meat is hidden inside a folded piece of dough. This makes it possible to serve *Maultaschen* during the fasting period, as the Lord above cannot see the meat! The meat is minced finely, mixed with spinach, and wrapped in its cloak of dough. It is still a traditional dish served throughout the region on Maundy Thursday.
A limerick featuring the *Maultasche* fairly sums up the Swabian view of this doughy delicacy:

> The Swabian idea of
> repasting,
> Is to eat something solid and
> lasting.
> The Maultasche of pork
> Will adorn any fork,
> And is just what you need
> when you're fasting.

FISH FOR A KING FROM THE "SWABIAN OCEAN"

Despite its nickname, the "Swabian Ocean" is, of course, composed of sweet, rather than salt, water. So anyone expecting that the fish referred to in the headline might be sole or cod will be disappointed at first – but not once he has tasted them! The "Swabian Ocean" is identical with Lake Constance, and two of the best fish served in Swabia flourish in it: the whitefish, called *Felchen* in Swabia and *Renke* in other parts of south Germany, and the trout. Fish fans in the south of Germany divide into two camps: those who favour the trout and those who favour the *Felchen* or *Renke*. The *Felchen* fans claim that it is less bland than the trout, while trout lovers regard their favourite as more delicate in taste and texture, characteristics which become more noticeable when the fish are smoked.

Throughout the ages fish has been a prominent item in man's diet, and has played a particularly important part in Catholic areas as it could be eaten on Fridays, for example, in lieu of forbidden meats, for which reason many monasteries had their own fish ponds. This distinction between fish and meat led, probably during the Reformation, to the saying "neither fish nor flesh", meaning people who did not wish to commit themselves fully to Catholicism or Protestantism: the Catholics had to fast on Fridays, but could eat fish, while the Protestants were allowed to eat meat. The theme "Food and Religion" is no longer of topical interest these days, and is ignored by most people. So let us get away from it, and see what the fish market has to offer.

Felchen: a member of the whitefish group in Central European lakes, 18 per cent protein, 3 per cent fat, tasty flesh resembling that of the trout.

Trout: a predatory fresh water fish, 20 per cent protein, 3 per cent fat, white, sometimes pinkish flesh, with few bones. There are brown trout, salmon trout, and rainbow trout. The rainbow trout, which was introduced from North America, grows fast, and is ideal for fish farms.

Although the water quality of Lake Constance has steadily improved in recent years, there are seven fish-breeding establishments on its shores to keep up stock. About a million fish eggs, mainly whitefish, but also trout, grayling, and pike, are introduced

when winter is over into the "Swabian Ocean", as the lake is sometimes called. More than two hundred part-time fishermen harvest the waters.

In 1991 nearly 12,000 tons of fish were landed, about 730 of which were whitefish. "Honau, Hauff, and fresh-caught fish – with trout enough for all . . ." – a Swabian catch-phrase to lead us into the next story. An outing to Honau, a village to the south of Reutlingen, has always been a favourite with the Swabians, and to lunch or dine on fish is an essential part of the trip. To walk up the hill to Lichtenstein Castle,

made famous by Wilhelm Hauff's novel "Lichtenstein", published in 1829, and then to sit in the Adler Hotel with a view of the Castle and the menu in front of one, is a life-enhancing experience for all those who also take a delight in culinary things. If you sit in the hotel garden, you can watch the objects of your desire swimming in the waters of the young Echaz River – before they take their last swim in a choice Riesling sauce.

The menu includes 10 trout dishes. For four generations, the Walker family has spoilt their guests, and prospered in the

Before the fish lands on the table it has been poached, fried, or (as on the left), smoked.
The two fishermen on the Upper Neckar are unlikely to be hoping for a rare brown trout. What usually lands on the plate is a rainbow trout.

Walter Dietmayer disclosed to us his recipe for a tasty fish sausage: Take
1 kg of fillet of grayling,
2 eggs, 1 bread roll,
1 bunch of parsley, salt, pepper, and marjoram.
Pass the fish fillet through a mincer, mix it with all the other ingredients, thickening if necessary with breadcrumbs.
Mould into sausage shape, and place the skinless sausage in boiling water to simmer until it floats to the surface.
The sausage goes well with bread, fried in lard, with potato salad, or simply on its own...

process. The village inn has transmuted into an hotel where the family serve their guests with a liveliness reminiscent of the swift movements of the trout in the water.

The Adler trout are baptized in two different waters. Raised in a pool near Gammertingen-Hettingen in water from Sebastian's Spring, they are subsequently seasoned, as it were, in the waters of the Echaz.

The trout are bred by Walter Dietmayer, who makes sure that the Walkers are never short of fresh fish. The rainbow trout from Hettingen are transferred alive to the Echaz, and guests can watch the cook fishing for their meals.

With a temperature of only 9 °C, Sebastian's Spring ensures that the Dietmayer trout and grayling become firm and muscular, because the fish do not grow so fast in cold water. It takes two years before they have attained the right size for a single portion: between 380 and 400 grams. During this time the trout will have eaten up to 2 or 3 kilos of feed. It would be a mistake for the breeder to give them more: trout have to be kept on short commons, otherwise they overeat

until they burst. And during breeding the small fish must be kept separate from the adults, who would otherwise devour them. But the many guests at the Adler do not concern themselves about such things. The fish in the kitchen basin in the Echaz are all equal in size and quality. On good days, two hundred are served – whole or filletted, in Riesling or champagne, fried or smoked, in dill or saffron sauce, as soup, pie, or in aspic.

And so the lively life of the trout is sacrificed to delight the palates of the trippers. Yes, little fish are sweet, as the proverb goes . . .

Fishing with a rod is a slow game. Like other breeders, Walter Dietmayer nets his trout and grayling from the basin. Before a grayling reaches a commercially interesting size, it will have eaten one and half to twice its final weight in feed.

45

IN VINO VERITAS – THE TRUTH AT LAST!

To pour wine down your gullet is to sin.
To drink wine is to pray!
(Theodor Heuss, former Federal President of West Germany)

Right: Here, directly behind the Tübingen Town Hall, the "Gogei" begins – the old part of town that was once inhabited almost solely by wine-growers. Much has changed in the meantime. The houses have been done up, the odd boutique has been opened, and rough-hewn, earthy characters, once typical of the quarter, have become a rarity. Tübingen wines have also become rare. They used to be dubbed "throat-scrubbers" by the students, but today they are respectable table wines.

And now let us pray that the wine develops the way it should – and if it does, not only will the connoisseurs thank us. For today's beginners are tomorrow's experts. A taste for wine takes a lifetime to develop, is passed on through generations, needs constant attention and nursing. Wine has to be approached slowly, must be nosed, tasted, felt. It is a sin to shock wine, to handle it roughly, to shake it, to knock it, or simply to gulp it down without thought. Wine is not merely a drink – wine is culture, philosophy, discernment. "Who is he telling this to?" – some readers may ask. Wine lovers have philosophized on this point ever since we have had wine, and we have had it, thank God, for centuries. It was brought to us by the Romans, and was later tended and coddled by the monks. The monks not only coddled it, they were great tipplers on occasion, and other privileged persons never went short of it, while the common folk had to be satisfied with poor-man's wine: cider. Now, after decades of prosperity, during which the fermented juice of the apple or pear was regarded as too lowly a drink, it is gradually becoming fashionable to get a bottle of cider up from the cellar for one's guests; and, of course, it can also be used for cooking.
On the wine front, the growers are having to fight for survival today in increasingly competitive markets, and one can only wish them well. After all, a mere ten per cent of their product consists of nutrients – the other ninety per cent is sheer enjoyment! Enjoyment packed at first in the form of Trollinger, Lemberger, Schwarzriesling, Riesling, or Kerner grapes, for example, that grow along the Swabian Wine Route, enjoyment that can also, I hope, be anticipated when reading relatively dry information such as this.
The River Neckar and its tributaries Rems, Murr and Bottwar, Enz, Zaber, Kocher, and Jagst, are the arteries of the Swabian wine region, in which red wines dominate. Almost 2,000 of the 8,500 hectares are devoted to the Trollinger, which chiefly yields a robust wine ideal to go with elevenses or with a mid-afternoon bite – or *Vesper*, as such snacks are called in Swabia. Among the choice wines we find the Lemberger, and the Schwarzriesling more often than the Trollinger – which is also known

In the area where Swabia gives way to Franconia, the Neckar forms some impressive bends, as here near Kirchheim. The sunny slopes along the river produce fine vintages year after year.

by a number of other names, such as Tirolinger and Gross-vernatsch. The Trollinger grape probably came to Swabia from the Tirol, where it is used in Merano, for example, for grape-cures.

Among the white wines, the Riesling leads the way quantity-wise, followed by the Silvaner. Among the choicest local wines, the "treasure-chest" bottles, the Riesling and, as a true child of "greater Swabia", the Kerner, deserve special attention.

It is said that in the old days the wine-grower walked around his vine seventeen times during the course of the year, concluding his work after the harvest by tidying and protecting the vines against the approaching winter. Some of the processes are scarcely known by the younger generation of viti-culturists. Mechanization, and changes in production methods have made the wine-grower's work easier, but it is still tough enough. Wine enlivens the spirits, but earning one's living by it is an exhausting business. A steep slope cannot change its nature, and even rationalization cannot always make "the crooked straight and the rough places smooth". Anyone who has taken

Trollinger grapes, the basis for what is by far the most-drunk, and perhaps the best-loved, of all wines consumed in this region.

part in the grape harvest knows that it is back-breaking work and that the wine-grower earns his living the hard way. It would do every wine-lover good to work at least once in his life as a picker and learn to appreciate the amount of effort that goes into only one of the phases of turning grapes into the elixir of life. And if one remembers that the wine-grower not only invests so much work in his product but is actually prepared – at a price, of course – to part with it in the end, one can only agree with Omar Khayyám, when he says in his Rubáiyát:

> I wonder often what the Vintners buy
> One half so precious as the stuff they sell.

Terraced vineyards have a poetic quality which enables the on-looker to forget the hard work they entail, and walking through such an area is like walking through a genre painting – except that there is the added delight of anticipating arriving at one of the many taverns which are often no more than the front parlour of the wine-grower's house. The broom hung outside is a signal that there is something worth drinking inside – *Federweisser*, or new wine; new wine that can have shattering effects on the digestive tract of the unwary or incautious. An experienced *Federweisser* drinker once said to me: "If I got a mark for every potential hangover carried home by new-wine drinkers, I could spend the rest of my life downing champagne!"

For the wine-grower, running a tavern can be a profitable business, because apart from the many glasses of wine consumed, happy drinkers usually want some kind of a foundation for it in the form of food. The strain of the harvest is quickly forgotten at least by the host once the broom signifying that *Federweisser* is being served has been hung outside the tavern, although he certainly needs considerable fortitude of mind and body to survive the season without damage to the one or the other. But the continuous ringing of the till through the long nights is such sweet music in the host's ears that he willingly postpones his sleep till the following day.

In addition to the dyed-in-the-wool tavern-keepers, there are also other producers in Swabia

who sell bottled wine direct to the consumer, and whose often considerable output of good quality wines gives them independence, adds colour and interest to the market, and enhances the reputation of Württemberg wines. Most wine-producers, however, are organized in co-operatives, which is understandable in a region where the great majority of vineyards are small, belonging mainly to farmers, and even to part-time growers. The cooperatives look after their members – and their wine – extremely well up to the point when it finds its way into our cellars and glasses, and we can drink to a good vintage, recent or remote.

Simply knowing how much pleasure and fun will one day emerge from such a barrel will hardly be enough to keep our cooper happy. His good mood is probably a result of the change in the market situation: wooden barrels are coming in again.

Metamorphosis
Blessed unnumbered times
by the dew of the heavens
and the earth's vitality,
the sap rises in the vine.
And into its golden wine
draws sun, moon, and
stars.

So as he sips,
the gentle drinker
drinks
the dew of the heavens
and the earth's vitality,
and in his golden wine
finds starlight and sun-
shine.
(August Lämmle)

Wherever wine grows it is
also drunk with pleasure,
at quiet moments, in con-
vivial company – and, of
course, with a good meal.
Some of the dishes de-
scribed in the following
pages may well be en-
hanced or perfected by
being accompanied by a
glass of wine. Just in case
that's the case, here's to
your health . . . !

PS:
The British and American
weights and measures
given in the brackets in
the recipes are the nearest
practical equivalents of the
metric figures.

GLOSSARY

There are a few terms used in Swabian cookery which are untranslatable, in that they describe dishes which are unique to this area of Germany, or which are so typical that to render them into English would be like trying to cook a curry without the right spices or a garlic soup without the garlic.

The first that springs to mind is:

Spätzle: The Swabian "national dish", consisting of pasta, slivers of which are scraped off a board, or passed through a special grater, into boiling water.

Maultaschen: The Swabian answer to ravioli.

Knöpfle: Small light dumplings (literally "small buttons").

Flädle: Thin pancakes, cut into strips and added to some soups.

Küchle: Small tarts or cakes.

The diminutive le or la, accompanied by the addition of umlauts to preceding vowels (a,o, and u), and liberally used in Swabian, is appended to many food and cookery terms, so that, for example, *Haxe* (leg), becomes *Häxle, Knopf* (button) *Knöpfle*, and *Rad* (wheel) *Rädle*.

For more detailed descriptions, see the individual recipes.

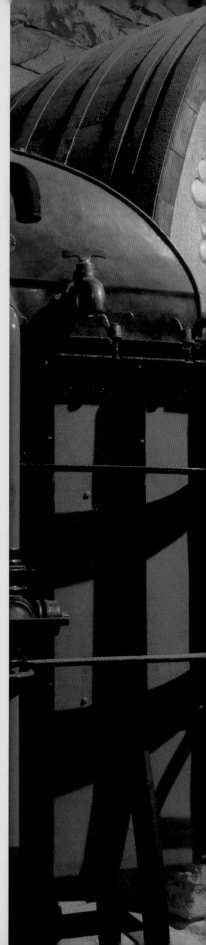

SNACKS, STARTERS, SALADS, AND SOUPS

ELEVENSES

4 marrow bones
600 g (1¼ lb) lean brisket of beef
1 onion
1 bay leaf
2 cloves
1 clove of garlic
1 veal tongue
200 g (½ lb) calf's sweet-breads
1 carrot
1 leek
1 small celeriac
a little butter

Boil some salted water. Put in the marrow bones, and brisket. Simmer for 2–2½ hours. Skim. Add onion, bay leaf, cloves, and garlic. In the meantime put the tongue into cold water and bring to the boil; simmer for 2 hours.

Blanch the sweetbreads, remove skin and blood clots.

Wash the carrot, leek, and celeriac, peel and cut into thin strips. Sauté in a shallow pot in butter on a low flame.

Take the cooked tongue from the water, and remove skin while still warm. Add the tongue and sweetbreads to the brisket, and simmer for about a further 20 minutes. Test with fork for tenderness.

Serve with the sautéed vegetables, grated horseradish mixed with cream, and brown bread or fried potatoes.

One of the features of life in Swabia is the "Frühschoppen", the mid-morning glass of wine, cider, or beer, accompanied by a snack which may include any of a variety of hot dishes – various boiled meats, pig's kidneys in a sour sauce, a plate of tripe, perhaps.

It should be pointed out that the use of the word "Vesper" for snack does not indicate that it can only be eaten in the evening: any time between 0 and 24 hours is just right.

SWABIAN POTATO SALAD

Potato flowers: miniature beauties.

1 kg (2¼ lb) waxy potatoes
1 onion
salt, freshly-milled pepper
1 teaspoon mustard
2 tablespoons wine vinegar
1 cup broth
3 tablespoons sunflower
or other vegetable oil

NB:
*Use only best waxy
potatoes.*
*Potato salad should be
eaten on the day it is made.
Never serve it straight
from the fridge – it is
tastier if it is not too cold.*

Wash the potatoes in their
jackets, and boil in not too salty
water. Peel while still warm, cut
into thickish slices. Add the diced
onion, salt, pepper, mustard,
vinegar, broth, and oil, and mix.
Leave to steep, and then taste for
seasoning.
Serve with warm Swabian or
Bavarian-style meat loaf, with
sausages of your choice, or whatever you fancy. It goes down well
with a glass of Trollinger or a cool
beer.

A Swabian without "Spätzle"
and his special version of
*potato salad is unthinkable.
There are a number of variations
on this special version – some
people add thinly sliced fresh
cucumber, for example, or use
grated instead of sliced potatoes
for it.
For the version with grated
potatoes, grandmother's recipe
calls for the yolks of two hard-
boiled eggs. The potatoes, boiled
the previous day, are peeled and
grated; add finely chopped onion,
salt and pepper, mix the egg yolk
with vinegar and pour over the
potatoes together with the lukewarm broth. Stir the oil in,
mixing well.*

BACON FLAN

There's nowt better than sum-mat good! And bacon flan certainly qualifies as good. Serve it to your friends during an evening party, together with a dry Trollinger or Riesling.
A popular variation is bacon and leek flan. For this version take only 30 g (1 oz) of bacon and add 150 g (5 oz) of coarsely chopped leek.

The dough:
180 g (6½ oz) plain flour
10 g (⅓ oz) yeast
125 ml (4½ fl oz) luke-warm water
2 tablespoons oil
salt

For topping:
80 g (3 oz) butter
2 egg yolks
200 g (½ lb) sour cream
150 g (5 oz) bacon
100 g (¼ lb) onion
10 g (½ tablespoon) cara-way seeds

Fat for the baking sheet

Put the flour in a bowl. Dissolve the yeast in the water, add the oil and a pinch of salt. Pour the mixture into a well formed in the centre of the flour; mix and knead into a smooth dough. Put in a warm place to rise.
Preheat the oven to 200 °C (400 °F). In the meantime cream the butter, then gradually stir in the egg yolks and sour cream. Chop the bacon and onions well; add caraway seeds.
Knead the dough again for a short time, roll out into a thin sheet, place on the greased baking sheet, and spread the topping on the dough. Bake for about 18 minutes, with heat mainly from below.

Swabian Meat Soup
Chick Cheese

CHICK CHEESE (below)
Whip the cream well, and mix it with the cottage cheese and the sour cream. Season with salt and pepper, and scatter the caraway seeds and chopped chives over it.

*I*n Swabian "Luckele" means chicks, but what have chicks to do with this simple cottage cheese dish, the reader may ask. The answer: chicks used to be fed with this kind of cheese – unseasoned, of course. But properly seasoned it certainly does not taste like chicken feed – served with new potatoes, it is a dish not to be pecked at.
And anyone who has a colander of the kind shown in the small picture, can make the cottage cheese for this white delicacy him/herself.

SWABIAN MEAT SOUP
200 g (½ lb) calf's head
200 g (½ lb) ox muzzle salad
200 g (½ lb) galantine of pork
1 red onion
1 bunch radishes
1 small bunch chives
The dressing:
3 tablespoons sunflower or other vegetable oil
1 tablespoon cider vinegar
100 ml (4 fl oz) cider
1 teaspoon medium-hot mustard
salt, pepper, pinch of sugar

CHICK CHEESE
100 ml (4 fl oz) cream
800 g (1¾ lb) cottage cheese
100 g (4 oz) sour cream
salt, pepper, caraway seeds, 1 bunch chives

SWABIAN MEAT SOUP (above)
Cut the boiled calf's head meat, the ox muzzle salad, and the galantine into bite-sized pieces. Finely slice the onion and radishes and mix with the freshly chopped chives. Mix the dressing ingredients well, and carefully stir into the "soup".

*Y*ou will already have noticed that this is not what is usually understood by the word "soup" – but is actually a substantial and tasty, very Swabian, meat salad. Serve it on a warm summer's evening together with fried potatoes.

SUCKING PIG IN ASPIC

400 g (1 lb) shoulder of
sucking pig
5 litres (8⅓ pints) of water
100 g (4 oz) pickling salt
1 onion
1 bay leaf
1 clove
30 g (1 oz) carrot
30 g (1 oz) courgette
30 g (1 oz) pickled gherkin
125 ml (4½ fl oz) gherkin
pickling liquid
125 ml (4½ fl oz) brine
from the sucking pig
20 g (⅔ oz) aspic powder

The onion dressing:
1 egg yolk
3 tablespoons sunflower or
other vegetable oil
2 tablespoons cider vinegar
1 tablespoon cider
1 teaspoon medium-hot
mustard
salt, freshly-milled pepper
pinch of sugar
2 onions
1 small bunch chives

Hard-boiled eggs for
garnishing

NB:
*Ask your butcher to bone
the meat.
On hot summer days the
amount of aspic powder
should be increased by
2–3 grams.*

Steep the boned meat in the
water with pickling salt for
2–3 days in a cool place. Remove
from the brine, setting 125 ml
(4½ fl oz) of brine aside.
Cook the meat in unsalted water
for 2–2½ hours together with
the onion, bay leaf, and clove.
Take the meat out; when cold cut
into small cubes. Dice the carrot
and courgette, blanch. Slice the
gherkin finely and arrange in four
soup cups with the other ingredients. Mix the gherkin pickling
liquid and meat brine and boil up
with the aspic, stirring all the
time. Allow to cool somewhat
and pour into the cups. Cool further for about 8 hours in the
fridge. Then dip the cups briefly
in hot water, turn out the con-
tents onto plates, and add the
onion dressing after garnishing
with slices of hard-boiled egg.
For the onion dressing the ingredients should be mixed well with a
blender, adding the chopped onions and chives last.

*A*nother dish suitable for
elevenses – no matter at
*what the time of day. Pretzels
and a glass of dry red or white
wine go down well with it.*

BEAN SALAD WITH CALF'S KIDNEYS

500 g (1 lb) of wax beans

The dressing:
1 onion
1 small bunch parsley
2 tablespoons wine vinegar
3 tablespoons sunflower or
other vegetable oil
1 teaspoon medium-hot
mustard
1 teaspoon sugar
salt, freshly-milled pepper

2–3 calf's kidneys
salt, freshly-milled pepper
1 tablespoon plain flour
1 tablespoon oil

The horseradish butter:
80 g (3 oz) butter
50 g (2 oz) grated horse-
radish
lemon juice

The garnish:
2 tomatoes
50 g (2 oz) cress

Wash the beans, cut away the
stringy edges if necessary, boil,
drain, and cool.
For the dressing, chop the onions
and parsley. Mix with the other
ingredients. Add the beans
2–3 hours before serving.
Clean the kidneys and trim off
the fat, slice them and season
with salt and pepper.
Dust with flour and lightly fry in
oil.
Cream the butter and horseradish, adding a few drops of
lemon juice.
Garnish with quartered tomatoes,
the cress, and the horseradish
butter.

*A light snack for a summer eve-
ning. A dry Riesling, possibly
with a dash of mineral water
added, and a slice or two of
brown bread make an ideal
accompaniment.
Liver or sweetbreads can be
served instead of the kidneys.*

Cabbage Salad with Fillets of Duckling

The Swabians used to live very simply as there would otherwise not have been enough to go around. But times have changed – and the old cliché about the homespun Swabian cuisine no longer applies.
And yet, of course, the soil in the Swabian Uplands is just as thin as ever, and farmers still have regularly to gather up the stones that constantly rise to the surface so as to make best use of their fields.

1 small head of red cabbage
salt and pepper
1 onion
3 tablespoons Balsamico vinegar
2 tablespoons redcurrant jelly
2 cooking apples
3 tablespoons walnut oil

4 breasts of duckling
salt and pepper
1 tablespoon oil

NB:
Red cabbage, rich in vitamins, is an ideal winter dish.
The cabbage can be shredded with a meat or bread slicer.

Remove the outer leaves, coarse ribs, and core. Shred the cabbage into a bowl and add salt and pepper. Put aside for 2 hours, then add the chopped onion.
Preheat oven to 180 °C (350 °F). Warm the vinegar and redcurrant jelly slightly, pour over the cabbage, and allow to steep while peeling and cutting up the apples into small pieces. Then mix the apple and oil with the cabbage. Season the breasts of duckling with salt and pepper, fry quickly on a high flame, finishing with about 15 minutes in the oven. Allow to stand for a few minutes before slicing.

SWABIAN CIDER SOUP WITH CALF'S HEAD

200 g (½ lb) calf's head meat
½ onion
1 clove, and 1 bay leaf
salt

300 g (¾ lb) veal bones
100 g (4 oz) onions
20 g (1 oz) celeriac
40 g (1½ oz) leeks, white part only
1 apple
2 tablespoons oil
250 ml (9 fl oz) cider
250 ml (9 fl oz) white wine
½ litre (¾ pint) of the liquid the head was boiled in
½ bay leaf
3 juniper berries
1 clove
1 tablespoon cornflour
200 ml (7 fl oz) cream
sugar, salt, glutamate

NB:
The rest of the meat from the calf's head can be used for a tasty salad the next day:
Slice the meat thinly, and dress with wine vinegar, oil, thinly sliced onions, salt and pepper.
Arrange on lettuce leaves, garnish with radishes and scatter chopped chives over it. Serve with bread or fried potatoes.

Cook the meat together with the onion, clove, and bay leaf in salted water for a good 2½ hours till really tender.

In the meantime chop the bones small, fry them in the oil together with the sliced onions, celeriac, leeks, and apple, without browning. Pour the cider in and top up with a third of the white wine and the liquid in which the calf's head was boiled. Add the herbs and seasoning, and boil well.

Strain the soup and boil up again. Mix the cornflour with a little of the white wine, and stir into the boiling soup with the rest of the wine. Finally add the cream, boil up once more, and season with sugar, salt and glutamate.

Cut the boiled calf's head meat into small cubes, and add to the soup.

A pple or pear cider is called "Most" in Swabia – the equivalent of the English word "must" – and usually denotes still cider. It can, of course, be drunk, as well as cooked with! It used to be the poor man's wine, but has become more respectable of late.

BREAD SOUP

Bread soup has gone out of fashion, but it is really the most sensible way of using left-over bread. And the idea that the Swabian housewife will not allow a clove of garlic into her kitchen, or that her husband takes objection to the smell, is now quite out of date: travel has broadened their minds in this respect at least. The crushed garlic adds a sniff of the great wide world to this soup, giving it an exotic touch that makes all the difference.

100 g (4 oz) of left-over bread
60 g (2 oz) butter
1 onion
1 tablespoon plain flour
1½ litres (2½ pints) broth
1 clove of garlic
2 egg yolks
3 tablespoons cream
salt, freshly-milled pepper
nutmeg
1 slice white bread
1 slice brown bread
1 bunch chives

Fry the thinly sliced bread in some melted butter in a large pot till golden.
Add the diced onion and fry a little longer. Dust with flour, stir, and add the now cool broth. Put in the crushed clove of garlic, bring the soup to the boil, and simmer for 20 to 30 minutes.
Beat the egg yolks and cream in a tureen, and pour in the hot soup. Season with salt, pepper, and nutmeg.
Dice the 2 slices of bread, fry quickly, and scatter on the soup with the chopped chives.

VARIOUS SMALL DUMPLINGS

BRAIN DUMPLINGS
1 shallot
60 g (2 oz) butter
2 egg yolks
70 g (2½ oz) boiled brain
1 tablespoon parsley
1 tablespoon chives

COTTAGE CHEESE
DUMPLINGS
40 g (1½ oz) butter
2 egg yolks
50 g (2 oz) breadcrumbs
80 g (3 oz) cottage cheese
(40 % fat)
1 teaspoon finely chopped
basil
salt, pepper, nutmeg

HERB DUMPLINGS
1 medium-sized onion
2 bunches (50 g/2 oz)
parsley
1 bunch chives
20 g (⅔ oz) butter
2 slices of white bread
125 ml (4½ fl oz) milk
2 eggs
1 bunch chervil

The Spätzle dough:
300 g (11 oz) plain flour
3 eggs
125 ml (4½ fl oz) water

Nutmeg, salt, pepper

BRAIN DUMPLINGS (top)
Dice the shallot, fry without
browning in a dab of butter, and
allow to get cold.
Cream the rest of the butter and
gradually stir in the egg yolks.
Squeeze the brains dry; stir into
the butter/egg yolk together with
the shallot, chopped parsley, and
chives.
Scoop teaspoonfuls out of the
mixture, each time dipping the
spoon first into cold water, and
place the little dumplings on a
baking sheet. Bring salted water
to the boil, drop the dumplings
in, bring up to the boil again, and
poach on a very low flame for
about ten minutes.

COTTAGE CHEESE DUMPLINGS
(middle)
Cream the butter. Gradually add
the egg yolks and breadcrumbs.
Squeeze the cheese dry and add
to the mixture together with the
basil. Keep in a cool place for
about an hour.
Now proceed as above for Brain
Dumplings.

HERB DUMPLINGS (below)
Cut the onion in thin slices.
Wash and chop the parsley and
chives. Fry the onion and herbs
without browning, and allow to

get cold. Dice the crust of the
bread and the crumb separately.
Bring the milk to the boil and
soak the diced crust in it. Mix the
diced crumb with the eggs.
Make the Spätzle dough. Mince
the now cold onion and herbs
together with the soaked crust
and the egg/crumb mixture, and
add to the Spätzle dough; mix
well and taste for seasoning.
Drop spoonsful of the mixture in
boiling salted water and boil until
they rise to the surface. Lift out
carefully with a slotted spoon,
and drain on a flat strainer.

*A home-made broth of beef
and marrow bones with de-
licious, light dumplings – what a
treat! The dumplings also make
an excellent garnish for many
meat dishes.*

CARROT SOUP WITH SEMOLINA DUMPLINGS

The dumplings:
20 g (⅔ oz) butter
1 egg
45 g (2 oz) semolina
salt, nutmeg

The soup:
500 g (1 lb) new carrots
2 shallots
50 g (2 oz) butter
1 litre (1¾ pints) poultry
broth or consommé
3 tablespoons cream
sugar
salt
freshly-milled pepper
sparkling white wine

To make the semolina dumplings, cream the butter, gradually add the egg and semolina, stir well, season to taste, and put in a cool place for a while. Then scoop out dumplings from the mixture and drop into boiling salted water; bring to the boil, pour cold water in to stop the boiling process, and bring to the boil again; then poach for a few minutes.

For the soup, wash and peel the carrots, and slice thinly. Chop the shallots and fry lightly in butter. Add the carrots, and fry further without browning. Add the broth, and simmer for about 30 minutes. When the carrots are soft take them and the shallots from the liquid, mash and sieve them and return to the liquid. Add the cream, sugar, salt, and pepper to taste, plus a dash of sparkling white wine. Before serving put the dumplings in the soup.

The idea of using sparkling wine to enhance this soup is certainly new-fangled. Our grandmothers would not have dreamed of such an extravagance. A bottle of "Sekt" – the German version of champagne – only appeared on the table on high days and on holidays.

CONSOMMÉ OF VENISON WITH LIVER DUMPLINGS

The stock:
1 kg (2¼ lb) venison bones
fat for frying
1 onion
½ celeriac
1 carrot
125 ml (4½ fl oz) red wine
salt
6 peppercorns
1 bay leaf
1½ litres (3 pints) of water
150 g (5 oz) shin of beef
1 clove of garlic
5 sprigs of parsley
4 egg whites
2 tablespoons sherry

The dumplings:
100 g (4 oz) streaky pork
50 g (2 oz) venison liver
50 g (2 oz) venison
150 ml (5 fl oz) cream
2 tablespoons brandy
salt, freshly-milled pepper
50 g (2 oz) finely chopped pistachio nuts

NB:
This consommé is bound to enhance your reputation as a cook! If you cannot obtain venison liver, calf's liver will do.

Heat the fat; fry and brown the venison bones. Chop the onions, celeriac, and carrot finely, add to the bones and fry. Add the water and red wine in several stages, reducing each time. Put in the seasoning, the herbs, and the rest of the water; simmer for about 4–5 hours.

Strain through a sieve, saving the vegetables; allow the broth to cool.

Mince the shin of beef, the boiled vegetables, the garlic, and parsley, and mix well with the egg white. Put the mixture in the broth and slowly bring to the boil, stirring constantly. Simmer on a very low flame for about 1–2 hours, then strain through a cloth. Boil up again and add the sherry.

For the dumplings, mince the pork, liver, and venison, rub through a sieve, and cool by placing the bowl in another, larger bowl, containing ice cubes. Fold in the cream and the brandy. Season with salt and pepper, finally adding the chopped pistachio nuts.

Using a teaspoon, scoop out half-moon-shaped dumplings from the mixture, simmer for a short while in hot water, and serve in the consommé.

Chanterelle Soup
Swabian Pancake Soup

CHANTERELLE SOUP
3 shallots
40 g (1½ oz) butter
200 g (7 oz) chanterelles
1 teaspoon tomato purée
white wine
¼ clove garlic, ½ bay leaf
1 sprig each of thyme and
chervil, parsley
1/2 litre (1 pint) of broth,
300 ml (11 fl oz) cream
1 tablespoon cornflour
salt, sugar, pepper,
nutmeg, chives,
a little whipped cream

SWABIAN PANCAKE SOUP
The broth:
300 g (¾ lb) beef bones
500 g (1 lb) brisket of beef
salt, 1 carrot, ¼ celeriac
1 bay leaf, 2 juniper berries, 1 onion, 1 small leek
a few sprigs of lovage
nutmeg, freshly-milled
pepper, 1 clove garlic
small bunch chives

The pancakes:
250 ml (9 fl oz) milk
3 eggs
120 g (4½ oz) plain flour
pinch of salt, and of sugar
2 tablespoons butter for
frying

NB:
*Serve the brisket of beef as
a main dish with horse-
radish sauce and fried
potatoes.*

CHANTERELLE SOUP (below)
Peel and chop the shallots and fry
lightly in the butter. Add about
two thirds of the chanterelles and
fry further till golden, stirring in
the tomato purée at the same
time. Pour in a dash of white
wine. Add the garlic, bay leaf,
and the stalks of the herbs (chop
the leaves, and add later); top up
with broth and boil well. Stir in
the cream, boil up briefly again,
and thicken with the cornflour
mixed with some white wine.
Taste for seasoning, and blend in
the mixer. Pass through a sieve,
boil up again, add the finely
chopped leaves of the herbs and
the chopped chives, and put in
the remaining chanterelles, sliced
if large. Serve with a spoonful of
whipped cream.

THE PANCAKE SOUP (above)
Put the bones into cold water and
bring to the boil. Pour off the
water, clean the bones, put them
in fresh cold water and bring to
the boil again; then add the meat,
salt, carrot, celeriac, bay leaf, and
juniper berries; simmer for
2–2½ hours, skimming several
times. Fry the halved onion
on the cut surfaces on a high
flame and add to the broth,
together with the leek, for the

last 30 minutes. Take the meat
out when it is done.
Put the fresh lovage leaves in a
hair sieve, and scatter grated
nutmeg and ground pepper, plus
the crushed garlic clove, onto the
leaves. Ladle the soup, without
the sediment, through the sieve,
boil up again, and taste for
seasoning.
Mix the batter and fry thin pancakes. Allow them to cool, cut
into thin strips, and add to the
broth. Scatter chopped chives on
the soup and serve immediately.

*There really are people who
no longer know how good
home-made broth can taste, let
alone how to make it! But give
them one taste of this Swabian
Pancake Soup and they'll be
converted!*

SALMON TROUT IN GREEN NOODLE DOUGH

5 fillets of salmon trout
(120 g/4½ oz each)
2 tablespoons Noilly-Prat
(French vermouth)
1 lemon
salt, pepper, sugar
100 ml (4 fl oz) cream
1 bunch dill
green noodle dough (see
recipe on p. 140)
1 egg white

The Riesling sauce:
1 shallot
1 tablespoon butter
2 tablespoons Noilly-Prat
250 ml (9 fl oz) Riesling
300 ml (11 fl oz) cream
1 tablespoon cornflour
salt, lemon juice, sugar
1 tablespoon crème fraîche

NB:
*Sweet water fish should be
as fresh as possible, but it
can be kept for a day, if
necessary, in the fridge in
a covered porcelain dish.
Once cooked, fish should
be served straight away, as
it tends to dry out in the
oven, and fall to pieces if
left in the cooking water.
Raw fish deep-freezes
well.*

Remove skin and any bones from the salmon, wash and dab dry. Chop one of the fillets very fine, salt, stir in the Noilly-Prat, and freeze lightly in the deep freeze. In the meantime marinate the other fillets in lemon juice, season, and put in a cool place. Machine-mix the slightly frozen chopped fillet till it forms into a lump, then gradually add the cream, which should be cold. Chop the dill finely, and stir into the mixture; season as necessary. Put the finished mixture in a dish placed in a basin with ice-cubes. In the meantime roll out the noodle dough thinly (about a millimetre). Cut out 8 rectangles; spread enough of the mixture in the centre of 4 of the rectangles to accommodate a fillet, spreading the rest of the mixture evenly over the fish. Brush the dough still exposed with white of egg. Cover the 4 portions with the remaining 4 rectangles of dough, closing well, and squeeze the ends together as shown in the illustration. Put to one side until the sauce is ready.
For the sauce, lightly fry the finely chopped shallot, pour in the vermouth, top up with white wine, retaining a small amount for later.

Add the cream and boil up. Mix the cornflour with the remaining wine, and with it thicken the sauce somewhat. Add salt, lemon juice, and a little sugar to taste, and the crème fraîche.
Cook the prepared trout fillets in boiling salted water for 3–4 minutes.
Surround each fillet with a little of the sauce, serving the rest in a sauce boat.

According to the encyclo-paedia, the salmon trout lives in off-shore parts of the sea between Portugal and the White Sea. It is traditionally fished during its upstream migration to breed. But in many places genuine salmon trout is no longer easily available, so we often have to make do with what is called salmon trout, but which is in reality a rainbow trout especially bred and fed – with astonishing success – to provide salmon-like flesh.

GRAYLING IN SOUR CREAM AND BREADCRUMBS

*I*n Swabia we have two varieties of grayling (a member of the salmon family): the lake grayling, which occurs only in high mountain, and a few deep pre-Alpine, lakes. It is a lucky angler who manages to hook one of these rare fish. The river grayling can be found more frequently again, now that our rivers are becoming cleaner. It first came to us, by the way, a century or so ago from North America. Its delicately pink flesh is even finer than that of the trout. It is eaten fried or poached.

700 g (1 ½ lb) fillets of grayling
juice of ½ lemon
salt, pepper
1 bunch dill
1 bunch parsley
1 bunch chervil
4 tablespoons grated white bread without crust
60 g (2 oz) butter
100 g (4 oz) sour cream

Skin the boned grayling fillets, rinse under running cold water, and dab dry with kitchen paper. Squeeze the lemon juice over the fillets, season lightly, and put in a cool place.

Wash the fresh herbs, chop finely, and mix with the white breadcrumbs.

Fry the fillets on the skin side only in half the butter. After about 2 minutes, sprinkle the herbs and breadcrumbs on the fish, and pour the sour cream on. Continue to cook, pouring the rest of the melted butter on bit by bit.

Serve with buttered boiled potatoes, and with a glass of dry Kerner or a light rosé.

POACHED FILLET OF CATFISH

3 shallots
20 g (1 oz) butter
20 ml (1 fl oz) Noilly-Prat
(French vermouth)
125 ml (4½ fl oz) white
wine
600 ml (1 pint) fish stock
(basic recipe on p. 100)
50 g (2 oz) celeriac
50 g (2 oz) leek (white
part)
50 g (2 oz) carrots
50 g (2 oz) parsley roots
1 bay leaf
2 cloves
5 juniper berries
1 small bunch dill
750 g (1¾ lb) fillet of
catfish
juice of ½ lemon
salt and freshly-milled
pepper
sugar

The horseradish sauce:
400 ml (¾ pint) vegetable
stock
1 tablespoon freshly grated
horseradish
250 ml (9 fl oz) cream
1 tablespoon lemon juice
1 tablespoon cornflour
white wine
salt, sugar

NB:
*The fillets should be
poached on a very low
flame.*

Lightly fry the peeled and finely chopped shallots in the butter, add the vermouth, and top up with the wine and fish stock. Cut the vegetables into thin strips and add to the stock together with the seasoning and the stalks of the dill (keep the dill tips for garnishing). Simmer the vegetables in the stock, but do not allow them to become too soft. Moisten the catfish filets with lemon juice, and sprinkle with a little salt; put them into the boiling stock for 3–4 minutes; lift them out carefully, and finish cooking them in a shallow pan with a little of the stock on a low flame.
For the sauce, pass the stock through a sieve, add the horseradish and cream, and boil up. Mix the cornflour with a dash of white wine and the lemon juice, and add to the boiling sauce. Taste for seasoning.
"Float" the fillets on sauce poured onto the individual plates, garnishing with the vegetable strips and dill leaves. Serve with dry or semi-dry white wine.

*Y*ou have on your table the lar-gest European freshwater fish – though hopefully not one of the largest specimens. It is said that they run to weights of up to 5 hundredweight in the lower Danube, but the largest "Swabi-an" catfish was caught after the second world war near Donau-wörth: exactly 3 metres long and weighing 3 hundredweight – fine as a trophy, but no good for the kitchen, for this
nocturnal hunter is best eaten young. The Danubian catfish, or wels, as it is also called, is usually fried, grilled, or baked in pastry. But it is particularly tasty when poached as above!

SCRAMBLED EGG WITH LAKE CONSTANCE EEL

Actually, all eels fished out of Swabian waters should really be females, for it is only they who swim up the European rivers on their migration from the mid-Atlantic Sargasso Sea. The males stay in the coastal waters. But these days both males and females are "naturally" introduced into the streams and rivers – so that they can be caught and can contribute to our cuisine. And a river eel really is something special.

But the Lake Constance eels – the lake, locally called the "Swabian Ocean", is shown here near Langenargen during one of its by no means rare stormy phases – are also a worthwhile delicacy. Eggs and smoked eel are an excellent combination. Together with the potato fritters they make a simple dish which can be eaten throughout the year.

The potato fritters:
500 g (1 lb) potatoes
300 ml (½ pint) milk
3 tablespoons cream
6 eggs
3 tablespoons plain flour
salt, freshly-milled pepper
nutmeg
clarified butter for frying

The scrambled eggs:
2 shallots
30 g (1 oz) butter
200 g (½ lb) smoked eel
6 eggs
1 small bunch dill

Boil the potatoes in their jackets till soft; peel while still warm. Mash and allow to cool.
Then mix the mashed potatoes with the warm milk, adding the cream, eggs, and flour, plus salt, pepper and nutmeg to taste.
Allow to stand for 30 minutes. Form the fritters, fry them in clarified butter, and keep them warm.
Now peel the shallots, chop them, and fry lightly in butter. Add the eel, cut into pieces, and stir for a few moments. Pour the beaten eggs with the chopped dill tips onto the mixture, allow to firm up a little, and serve with the fritters.

MEAT AND
GAME DISHES

SOUR TRIPE

800 g (1¾ lb) tripe
100 g (4 oz) plain flour
60 g (2 oz) lard or oil
1 onion
1 tablespoon tomato purée
1 litre (1¾ pints) broth or
water
2 bay leaves
2 cloves
10 mustard seeds
1 clove of garlic
5 peppercorns
salt, sugar
4 tablespoons red wine
vinegar
125 ml (4½ fl oz)
Lemberger (red wine)

NB:
*Ask your butcher to cut
the tripe in strips for you.*

Boil the washed and cut tripe in salted water till done; pour the water away.

Make a golden-brown roux of flour and lard or oil. Then add the finely sliced onion and the tomato purée, top up with the broth or water, put in the herbs and seasoning, and boil for about 20 minutes. Add the vinegar and red wine to taste. Pass the resulting sauce through a sieve, add the tripe to it, and bring to the boil again.

Serve with fried potatoes. Slice potatoes which were cooked the day before, and fry golden brown in lard together with thinly sliced onions.

The already opened bottle of Lemberger can be put on the table – or cider, or beer . . . just as you like.

Tripe, once a popular working-man's dish in Britain, but now out of fashion there, is still a favourite in Swabia and in many other parts of Europe, particularly France.
But try the Italian version, too. For this you need a white roux. So do not allow the flour to brown, omit the tomato purée in our recipe, and use white instead of red wine. Finally sprinkle grated cheese on the tripe and bake in the oven or put under the grill. Use lashings of garlic!

BEEF IN RED WINE WITH SAUSAGE DUMPLINGS

The marinade:
1 apple, 1 onion
1 carrot, 1 leek
¼ celeriac
1/2 litre (1 pint)
Lemberger (red wine)
1 tablespoon balsamico
vinegar
125 ml (4½ fl oz) broth
2 bay leaves, 3 cloves
4 juniper berries
1 clove garlic
pinch of sugar
salt, and freshly-milled
pepper

1 kg (2¼ lb) shoulder of
beef
2 tablespoons oil
2 teaspoons tomato purée
plain flour for dusting
salt, freshly-milled pepper
125 ml (4½ fl oz) broth

The sausage dumplings:
1 bread roll
4 tablespoons milk
40 g (1½ oz) smoked
ham-sausage
½ onion
150 g (5 oz) plain flour
3 eggs
1 tablespoon chopped
parsley

NB:
*The marinade not only
gives this pot roast the
right flavour, but also ten-
derizes the meat.*

For the marinade, core and slice the apple, and chop the onion, carrot, leek, and celeriac.
Put these with the other marinade ingredients into a pot with a lid, and steep the shoulder of beef in it for 2–3 days, turning it several times.
Take out the meat, dab dry with kitchen paper, and fry to seal in a heavy pot with oil. Add the marinade vegetables, fry them for a short while, and put in the tomato purée. Add most of the marinade in two to three portions, reducing after each addition.
Dust the pot roast with flour, top up with the remaining marinade and the broth. Simmer, covered with a lid, for about 2 hours. Pass the sauce through a sieve, and taste for seasoning.

For the sausage dumplings, dice the bread roll and pour hot milk over it. Chop the sausage and onion, fry lightly, and then mix with the soaked roll, flour, eggs and parsley to form a dough. Scoop out dumplings with a spoon, and boil in salted water. This sustaining dish can be served with lamb's lettuce sprinkled with chopped hard-boiled egg.

STOCKS FOR SOUPS AND SAUCES

BROWN VEAL STOCK
(makes about 2 litres/3½ pints)
1 kg (2¼ lb) bones, chopped small, from the spine or shin
500 g (1 lb) beef tendons and trimmings
50 g (2 oz) uncooked, smoked ham
1 carrot
3 pieces of mushroom
1 onion
¼ celeriac
2 cloves garlic
250 ml (9 fl oz) dry white wine
2 litres (3½ pints) water or vegetable stock (not cabbage stock)
1 tablespoon tomato purée
2 tomatoes
1 small bunch chervil

FISH STOCK
500 g (1 lb) fish trimmings (bones and head) of barbel, whiting, turbot, or sole
2 shallots
3 mushrooms
1 small bouquet garni with plenty of parsley stalks, tarragon, thyme, and chervil
50 g (2 oz) butter
2 tablespoons peanut oil
250 ml (9 fl oz) dry white wine
1 litre (1¾ pints) water
cayenne pepper (red pepper)

BROWN VEAL STOCK (centre)
Stir the veal bones in a pot for about 15 minutes without fat on a hot flame. Add the beef tendons and trimmings, the diced ham, and the chopped vegetables, reducing heat so as not to brown the vegetables. Stir in the white wine, and reduce the liquid to a small quantity. Top up with the vegetable stock or water. Put in the tomato purée, the pipped tomatoes, and the herbs. Simmer for about 4 hours till the liquid has been reduced to about half, frequently skimming. Finally strain through a sieve.

LIGHT VEAL STOCK (below)
This is the basis for white sauces served with veal. It is made in the same way as the brown stock, but the bones are not heated in a pot as above, but blanched – i.e. put in boiling water and briefly cooked. Omit the tomato purée, but use twice the amount of fresh tomatoes.

GAME STOCK (not illustrated)
The method is largely the same as for brown veal stock. Instead of the veal and beef ingredients, bones and trimmings of game are used, and juniper berries and sage are added.

FISH STOCK (top)
Wash the fish bones and trimmings thoroughly and fry lightly with the chopped vegetables and the bouquet garni in butter and peanut oil, without browning. Pour in the white wine and reduce to almost nothing. Top up with the water and spice with a little red pepper. Simmer for about 20 minutes, skimming frequently. Do not cook for too long or the stock will become glutinous. Finally strain through a sieve.

*T*hat's the way the Swabian likes it: a soup to start with, and plenty of sauce with the roast. But what is the answer when no natural gravy is produced? The magic word is stock. But please do not thicken with flour! The proper way to thicken is to reduce, or boil down, as the Americans say. Shortly before serving, a little butter or cream can be added to obtain a smoother consistency, or, in the case of some sauces and soups, purée of vegetables.

BRAISED VEAL IN WINE SAUCE

*T*his is a light meal for hot summer days, so the accompanying drink should be light, too – perhaps a white wine with a dash of mineral water in it.

1 kg (2¼ lb) shoulder of veal
100 g (4 oz) finely chopped onion
80 g (3 oz) butter, salt
40 g (1½ oz) plain flour
200 ml (7 fl oz) dry white wine
1 litre (1¾ pints) broth or white veal stock (recipe on p. 100)
1 bay leaf, 2 cloves
3 juniper berries, sugar
freshly-milled pepper
juice of ½ lemon
1 egg yolk
125 ml (4½ fl oz) cream

NB:
When frying, make sure that the meat and flour do not brown. Do not boil the sauce after adding the egg yolk and cream, as it will otherwise curdle.

Remove the skin, tendons, and fat from the meat as far as possible, then cut in 30–40 g pieces. Fry the chopped onion lightly in the butter, add the meat cubes, salt, and fry lightly. Dust with flour, stir, pour the white wine over the whole, and top up with broth or veal stock. Season, and add lemon juice to taste. Bring to the boil, and then simmer gently for about 50 minutes till tender. Take out the meat cubes, bring the sauce to the boil briefly, stir in the egg yolk mixed with cream, and pass through a sieve. Return the meat to the sauce. Serve with broad noodles tossed in a little butter and lettuce or some similar salad. Recipes for home-made noodles are on page 140.

SWABIAN VEAL RAGOÛT

800 g (1¾ lb) shoulder of veal
salt, freshly-milled pepper
3 tablespoons oil
2 onions
1 tablespoon tomato purée
125 ml (4½ fl oz) Riesling (white wine)
2 tablespoons plain flour
1 litre (1¾ pints) white veal stock (recipe on p. 100), or water
muslim bag of herbs with:
1 bay leaf,
1 sprig of thyme,
8 peppercorns, and
1 clove of garlic
8 small carrots with part of the green stalks
8 parsley roots
4 spring onions
1 tablespoon butter
1 tablespoon whipped cream

Remove tendons from the meat, then cut it into cubes about 3 cm across, add salt and pepper, and brown in oil in a casserole. Add the finely chopped onions and the tomato purée. Pour the white wine over the whole, reduce, dust with flour, and brown again briefly.

Top up with veal stock or water, put in the bag of herbs, and simmer for 1½–2 hours.

Boil the peeled carrots with the stalks and the parsley roots briefly in salt water (al dente!). Dip in iced water. Wash the spring onions, remove part of the green, and split down the middle. Lightly fry the carrots, parsley roots, and spring onions in butter, season with salt and pepper, and keep in a warm place.

Shortly before the ragoût is tender, remove the bag of herbs, season to taste with salt and pepper, and stir in the cream.

Serve something special with this excellent veal ragoût – herb dumplings, for example (recipe on p. 74), and the vegetables as above.

Ragoûts are made of meat, game, poultry, or fish, etc, to which are added a selection of piquant ingredients such as mushrooms, truffles, various kinds of dumplings, choice vegetables, crayfish tails, and so on, in a well-flavoured sauce. Ragoût often also means a very concentrated, refined, thickish sauce containing sweetbreads, meat dumplings, soft carp roe, brain, cocks' combs, truffles, morels, mushrooms, etc, which is used as a garnish for boiled meat, poultry, whole fish, and similar dishes . . . and so on, and so on for another 31 lines in our 100-year-old cookery encyclopaedia, which, after the main definition, then describes no less than 44 recipes for ragoût – and none of them is from Swabia. Ours is!

SWEETBREADS WITH ASPARAGUS AND PANCAKES

400 g (14 oz) calf's sweet-breads
1 onion, stuck with a bay leaf and clove

2 kg (4½ lb) asparagus
1 teaspoon each of salt and sugar
a few drops of lemon juice

3 shallots
100 g (4 oz) butter
2 small carrots
1 small kohlrabi
salt and freshly-milled pepper
250 ml (9 fl oz) light veal stock (recipe on p. 100) or broth (recipe "Swabian Pancake Soup", on p. 80)

The pancakes:
ingredients as in recipe on p. 80
1 tablespoon crème fraîche
4 morels, preferably fresh
30 g (1 oz) plain flour
2 tablespoons dry Riesling (white wine)
1 bunch of wild chives

NB:
Adding salt, sugar, and lemon juice to the cooking water for asparagus is usually a good idea – but not for green asparagus, as it then turns an ugly grey colour. Do not throw away the asparagus liquid – it can always be used for a cream of asparagus soup the next day!

Soak the calf's sweetbreads for 6 hours in cold water, then boil up in salted water together with the onion, bay leaf, and clove, and simmer gently for 10 minutes; the centre should still be pink.

Remove all skin and tough parts, and divide into small pieces. Wash the asparagus, cut off the ends, and peel; tie into small bundles with white thread, and wrap in a damp cloth until you need it. Boil the ends with the peel, salt, sugar, and lemon juice in plenty of water for 10 minutes, and put to one side.

Gently fry the shallots in a low-sided pan in a little butter. Add the sweetbreads, the baby carrots, and the kohlrabi; season with salt and pepper, and pour half of the veal stock over the whole. Cover the pot and simmer gently for a few minutes.

While the ragoût is cooking, bring the bundled asparagus to the boil in the liquid from the ends and peel, and simmer for 20 minutes.

Make the pancake batter, and fry thin pancakes, keeping them warm till ready to serve.

Once the ragoût is done, remove the lid, and reduce the sauce twice; add the crème fraîche and the morels, and top up with the remaining veal stock. Finally, thicken the sauce by stirring in the rest of the butter which you have kneaded into the flour, taste for seasoning, and add the white wine. Sprinkle the finely chopped chives onto the sauce.

A t first sight, the preparation of this festive dish may seem rather complicated, but the various steps are all so clear and simple, that it is really quite easy – and well worth the effort! By the way: fresh asparagus can be deep-frozen for up to 3 months. It should first be peeled and wrapped in kitchen foil. To cook, put into boiling water while still frozen.

CALF'S SWEETBREADS WITH MOREL SAUCE

500 g (generous 1 lb) calf's
sweetbreads
1 onion stuck with a bay
leaf and two cloves
salt and freshly-milled pepper
1 tablespoon olive oil
40 g (1½ oz) salted butter
1 tablespoon plain flour

The morel sauce:
200 g (7 oz) fresh morels
2 shallots
20 g (1 oz) butter
100 ml (4 fl oz) white wine
300 ml (½ pint) veal stock
(recipe on p. 100)
200 g (7 oz) double crème
fraîche
salt and freshly-milled
pepper
lemon juice

Bring the sweetbreads to the boil
in slightly salted water together
with the onion stuck with cloves
and bay leaf. Simmer gently for
30 minutes, then skin and slice
them. Season with pepper. Heat
the oil and salted butter in a pan
till it foams. Dip the sweetbreads
in flour, and fry on both sides for
about five minutes. Add salt as
needed.
For the sauce, clean the morels,
wash several times, and drain
thoroughly. Chop the shallots
finely and fry lightly together
with the morels in some butter.
Add the white wine and veal
stock, and simmer for 5 minutes.
Take out the morels. Reduce the
liquid to less than half, add the
crème fraîche, and reduce a little
more. Sieve the sauce, and,
keeping the pot warm, gradually
stir the butter in. Put the morels
back in the sauce, boil up again,
season with salt and pepper, and
add lemon juice to taste.
The dish can be accompanied by
home-made noodles (recipe on
p.140), and with a choice light
wine.

*Gourmets are unanimous on
one thing: calf's sweetbreads
are really something special. The
sweetbread is the thymus gland,
which is well-developed in the
calf (and lamb), but withers in
the adult animal.
Fresh morels are to be had in the
spring. They should be thoroughly
washed in lukewarm water, as
there is usually some earth cling-
ing to them.
In a good morel year it is worth-
while drying them. To do this,
slice the cleaned morels thinly.
Then either string them on a
thread and allow to dry in the
sun for several days, or put them
in the oven at 50 °C (120 °F)
with the door slightly ajar for
24 hours, turning them over half
way through to stop them from
sticking to the baking sheet.*

CALF'S LIVER WITH LEMBERGER SAUCE

a glass of Lemberger, are the ideal accompaniments.

Lemberger is a full-bodied red wine, similar to Spät-burgunder. Readers may have come across it elsewhere under different names, such as "(Blauer) Limberger", "Blaufränkisch," or "Schwarzfränkisch".

8 slices of calf's liver
(150 g/5 oz each)
mixed seasoning: salt, and
1 pinch each of curry,
paprika, freshly-milled
pepper, thyme, estragon
80 g (3 oz) butter
4 tablespoons Lemberger
(red wine)
125 ml (4½ fl oz) of
brown veal stock (p. 100)

4 small pears
butter, sugar, coriander
250 ml (4½ fl oz) of white
wine

NB:
The mixture of salt, and a pinch each of curry and paprika is good for all dishes with offal, or variety meats; mixed like this it also keeps well if kept out of the light.

Remove the skin and larger veins from the liver. Wash, and carefully dab dry with kitchen paper. Season a little, and fry to a golden-brown in the foaming butter, basting frequently. Then sautée gently on a low flame under a lid until pink inside. Pour the red wine into the gravy, reduce somewhat, add the veal stock, and reduce again.

Thinly slice the pears. Heat some butter in a pan with a little sugar till light brown, add the pears, and flavour with coriander. Pour in the white wine, and simmer down for a while.

Arrange the liver on preheated plates, pour a little sauce on the meat, and garnish with the pears. Home-made Spätzle and, of course,

ROAST NECK OF PORK ESSLINGEN STYLE

1.2 kg (2¾ lb) neck of pork
salt, freshly-milled pepper
2 cloves of garlic
4 tablespoons oil
500 g (1 lb) neck-of-pork bones
flavouring vegetables:
80 g (3 oz) carrots,
80 g (3 oz) celeriac,
1 onion, 1 leek
2 bay leaves
8 peppercorns
1 tablespoon tomato purée
3 onions
4 eggs

NB:
When buying the meat, make sure that it is marbled – then it is bound to be juicy.

Rub the meat with salt, pepper, garlic, and oil; then wrap in foil and allow to steep for 6 hours. Preheat the oven to 200 °C/400 °F (for fan-assisted ovens to 180 °C/350 °F).
Fry the bones, chopped small, in oil in the baking dish briefly, place the meat on the bones, and roast in the oven for about 1½ hours, reducing the heat somewhat after roughly 30 minutes. Baste frequently. After a further 40–45 minutes add the chopped vegetables, the bay leaves, and the crushed peppercorns, allow to brown a little more, then pour in some water. Add more water whenever necessary for the rest of the cooking time.
Take the roast out of the oven, and put in a warm place. Put the baking dish on the stove, add the tomato purée and some water. Reduce the sauce to the required amount, then pass through a sieve and taste for seasoning.
Fry the thinly sliced onions till golden brown, and fry the eggs in a separate pan.
Cut the neck of pork in slices; garnish with the fried onions and eggs.
Serve with Spindele (recipe on p. 138), and a glass of cider.

The people of Esslingen (a charming old town east of Stuttgart), are nicknamed "Onions". There is a town legend to account for this strange sobriquet: The devil once appeared at Esslingen market and asked one of the stallholders for an apple. Despite his fine clothes, she recognized him for what he was from his cloven hooves – and handed him a juicy onion instead. He bit into it without looking, let out a cry of rage, and branded the proud citizens with this not very flattering moniker – a nickname straight from Old Nick! Esslingen wine, by the way, once had a high reputation in the region, and was exported as far as Salzburg and Vienna.

FILLET OF PORK IN A HERB AND MUSHROOM CRUST

Cook with a little oil in a casserole in the preheated oven for 25–30 minutes.

Suitable accompaniments are Bubespitzle (recipe on p. 138), and a dry Riesling.

*F*illets are the finest parts of any animal – and baked in a crust of mushrooms and herbs are even finer! And it is not even difficult to do.

500 g (generous 1 lb) fillet of pork (tenderloin)
salt, freshly-milled pepper
2 tablespoons oil
600 g (1 ¼ lb) spinach
50 g (2 oz) mushrooms
50 g (2 oz) chanterelles
15 g (½ oz) fat bacon
1 small onion
20 g (1 oz) parsley
20 g (1 oz) chives
250 g (9 oz) veal forcemeat
20 g (1 oz) crème fraîche
1 egg
1 clove of garlic
1–2 pig's cauls

NB:
You can order the pig's cauls (approx. 20x30cm) in advance at your butcher's. The fillet should be trimmed of tips and ends.

Season the fillet with salt and pepper, fry all round in oil, then allow to cool somewhat.

Clean, wash, and blanch the spinach, and put the individual leaves on kitchen paper to dry. Preheat the oven to about 180 °C (350 °F). Wash, clean, and chop the mushrooms finely. Fry briefly together with the finely diced bacon, chopped onion and chopped herbs. Mix well with the forcemeat, crème fraîche, and egg, and season with salt, pepper, and the finely chopped clove of garlic. Spread a pig's caul out for each fillet, place the spinach leaves on it, and spread the mushroom and herb forcemeat 1cm thick on the leaves. Place the fillet on the forcemeat and wrap in the caul.

SUCKING PIG CHOPS WITH ONION PURÉE

8 sucking pig chops
salt, freshly-milled pepper
2 tablespoons oil

The onion purée:
2 red onions
250 ml (9 fl oz) Lemberger
(red wine)
2 tablespoons balsamico
vinegar
salt, freshly-milled pepper
2 tablespoons not too-
sweet woodland honey
20 g (1 oz) butter

The savoy cabbage:
1 savoy cabbage
salt
30 g (1 oz) butter
4 shallots
2 tablespoons plain flour
125 ml (4½ fl oz) meat
broth
salt, pepper, nutmeg
4 tablespoons cream

NB:
*Place a sprig of thyme in
the pan while frying, and
the meat will absorb the
aroma.
The water for dipping the
cabbage in after blanching
should be very cold, so in
warm weather it is advis-
able to cool it down with
ice cubes.*

Season the chops with pepper and salt, pour a little oil over them, and put in the fridge about 3 hours before you need them. Chop the onions well, and fry lightly in a pan. Pour on the wine and vinegar, and cook until the onions take on a purée-like consistency. Season with salt and pepper, stir in the honey and the cold butter, and serve while still warm with the fried chops. Remove damaged leaves and stem from the cabbage, cut into chunks, and wash. Then cook quickly till soft in rapidly boiling water, dip into ice-cold water, and drain in a sieve. Mince coarsely. Melt butter in a low-sided pot, fry the diced shallots in it, dust with flour, and pour on the meat broth. Stir well, then add the cabbage. Season with salt, pepper, and nutmeg, add the cream, and boil up briefly, stirring all the time.

You will sometimes find "Onion marmalade" offered as a side-dish in better restaurants. But the Brussels authorities have defined "marmalade" as a sweet preserve for spreading on bread, made of citrus fruit – in other words as a form of jam made of oranges, lemons, or grapefruits; so as good Europeans we should no longer use the term when onions but no sugar are involved! But, after all, an onion by any other name would smell as sweet – so let us just sit down and enjoy this delicious and simple side-dish.

MEDALLIONS OF PORK WITH MUSHROOMS

2 shallots
200 g (7 oz) fresh mush-
rooms
100 g (4 oz) fresh boletus
40 g (1½ oz) butter
salt, freshly-milled pepper
50 g (2 oz) white bread
without crust
2 egg whites
½ bunch parsley

The au gratin potatoes:
½ clove of garlic
2 tablespoons butter
400 g (1 lb) potatoes
salt, pepper, nutmeg
marjoram
100 ml (4 fl oz) cream

12 small medallions of
pork
oil for frying
2 tablespoons butter
fresh thyme

NB:
*White of egg binds the
mushroom and breadcrumb
mixture.
The crust stays firm and is
nevertheless light. This
also applies to other dishes
in which it is used – lamb
in a herb crust, for ex-
ample.*

Preheat the oven to 180 °C
(350 °F). Briefly fry the finely
chopped shallots and mushrooms
in butter; season with pepper and
salt. Allow to cool somewhat, mix
with the white bread, rubbed
into crumbs, and the egg whites,
and add the chopped parsley.
Rub an oven-proof dish with the
garlic and brush it with butter.
Put the peeled and thinly sliced
potatoes in the dish in layers.
Pour on the cream, flavoured
with salt, pepper, nutmeg and
marjoram. Bake in the preheated
oven for about 20 minutes.
In the meantime, briefly fry the
medallions in oil, leaving them
pink in the middle, then arrange
on the pototoes, cover with the
mushroom mixture, distribute
dabs of butter on top, and put
back in the oven to crust over
lightly. Garnish with thyme.
A good accompaniment are fresh
summer vegetables such as peas
and carrots, or haricot beans
lightly sautéed in butter. A light
Müller-Thurgau is an ideal wine
to go with this delicately piquant
dish.

*The traditional Sunday lunch
in Swabia used to be roast
pork with "Spätzle" and a mixed
salad. Grandma would baste the
pork once more before leaving
for church, and take the smell of
the roast with her to her pew.
When the family came back from
the service shortly before noon
they would be able to sit down to
their meal more or less straight
away. Now the tendency is for
the family members to pursue
their various leisure activities
during the day, and to gather in
the evening for a meal and a
glass of something to round off
the week.*

LAMB CUTLETS WITH STUFFED TOMATOES

8 lamb chops
1 clove of garlic
1 sprig of thyme
freshly-milled pepper
125 ml (4½ fl oz) olive or
hazelnut oil
salt
20 g (1 oz) butter

The garlic butter:
120 g (4 oz) butter
salt, freshly-milled pepper
2 cloves of garlic
1 tablespoon chopped
parsley
1 tablespoon chopped
chives
a few drops of lemon juice
1 dash Worcester sauce

The stuffed tomatoes:
300 g (¾ lb) parsley roots
30 g (1 oz) butter
4 tomatoes
30 g (1 oz) crème fraîche
salt, freshly-milled pepper
nutmeg

NB:
*Garlic butter deep-freezes
well. First wrap in aluminium foil.*

Cut surplus fat off the chops, leaving only a thin border, and trim;
rub with garlic, thyme, and pepper. Place next to one another in
a pan, pour oil over them, and
keep in the fridge for 24 hours.
Drain the oil off just before frying,
salt them, and then fry briefly on
a moderate flame in a mixture of
oil and butter. Wrap them in
aluminium foil, and keep warm.
Before serving, garnish with a
slice of garlic butter.
To make the garlic butter: cream
the butter with the salt and pepper. Peel the garlic, and squeeze
through a press. Mix the parsley
and chives into the creamed butter, adding lemon juice and Worcester sauce to taste. Shape into a
roll in foil, and cool in the fridge.
For the stuffed tomatoes, wash,
peel and sauteé the parsley roots
in a shallow pan with some butter till they are soft. Dip the
tomatoes in boiling water, peel
them, and hollow them out with
a spoon. Mash the cooked parsley
roots, and rub through a sieve.
Put the purée in the mixer
together with the butter and
crème fraîche, mix well, adding
salt, pepper, and nutmeg to taste;
stuff the tomatoes with the mixture, and keep in a warm place
till ready to serve.

*In the old days, when we still
had an emperor, the shepherds
travelled with their sheep across
the Swabian Highlands in all
weathers, earning a meagre living
off the wool, which they sheared
twice a year. At that time most
people disdained mutton.
Now the few remaining shepherds still travel across country
with their flocks in all weathers,
but the price of wool is so low as
to be uneconomical. The little
they earn now comes from the
sale of lamb, which has become a
favourite meat with connoisseurs.*

KNUCKLES OF LAMB IN VINEGAR SAUCE

briefly in butter, and then add the sauce. Salt and pepper to taste, and possibly add another dash of red wine.

Spindele (recipe on p. 138) go well with this dish, and so does a glass of Trollinger, not too warm!

It is not surprising that lamb plays a significant role in the Swabian cuisine, since it is certainly comparable in quality to veal. Lambs (age limit one year) are ready for slaughter from as early as one month; the meat of two to three month old lambs is particularly good. The best cuts are the saddle and the legs.

4 knuckles of lamb
2 cloves of garlic
salt, freshly-milled pepper
2 tablespoons oil
250 ml (9 fl oz) Lemberger (red wine)
125 ml (4½ fl oz) red wine vinegar
1 leek
1 celeriac
1 carrot
2 onions
4 tomatoes
1 sprig rosemary
1 sprig thyme
2 bay leaves
5 peppercorns
20 g (1 oz) butter

Preheat the oven to 220°C/425 °F (fan-assisted ovens 180–200°C/ 350 °F–400 °F).
Cut the skin and tendons from the legs, and rub the legs with garlic, salt, and pepper. Fry all round in oil, then pour on the red wine and the red wine vinegar. Dice the leek, celeriac, carrot, and half an onion finely, add the tomatoes, cut into pieces, the rosemary, thyme, bay leaves, and peppercorns, and braise in the preheated oven for 1½–2 hours. Occasionally baste with a little red wine vinegar and water. Then take the meat out and keep hot. Top up the sauce with water and red wine, and allow to simmer for a while. Pass through a sieve. Chop the rest of the onions, fry

Saddle of Rabbit with Cider Sauce

4 saddles of rabbit à
200g (1/2 lb)

The sauce:
1 onion
40 g (1 1/2 oz) leeks, white
part only
1 apple
1 tablespoon olive oil
50 ml (2 fl oz) cider
70 ml (2 1/2 fl oz) white
wine
400 ml (3/4 pint) broth or
light veal stock (recipe on
p. 100)
1/4 clove of garlic
1 sprig of thyme
1 clove
5 juniper berries
200 ml (7 fl oz) cream
1 tablespoon cornflour
salt, sugar

The stuffing:
80 g (3 oz) grapes
60 g (2 oz) white bread
without crust
80 g (3 oz) crème fraîche
1 egg yolk
1 small bunch of chervil
salt, freshly milled-pepper
nutmeg
4 sheets of aluminium foil
(approx. 12" x 8")
20 g (1 oz) butter

Preheat the oven to 170 °C (325 °F). Cut the saddle meat out from below without damaging the skin on top – this enables the filets to be rolled more effectively. Leave the flanks on!

For the sauce, chop the bones into walnut-size pieces. Cut the onion, leek, and half the apple in cubes, and fry briefly with the bones in olive oil without browning. Pour the cider and three-quarters of the white wine into the pan, and top up with the broth or stock. Add the crushed garlic, the thyme, clove, and juniper berries, and simmer for about 1 hour. Begin making the stuffing about half way through the simmering time. For this, peel the grapes, remove the pips, and cut into small dice. Mix with the diced white bread and with the other ingredients, and season to taste. Butter the aluminium foil; place the filleted saddle, skin downwards, on the buttered foil. Spread the stuffing between the halves of the fillets. Roll the flanks round the stuffing to form a closed circle, and wrap the foil round each fillet, twisting the ends as in wrapped sweets. Bake in the oven for 15 minutes; take them out, and allow to rest for 3 minutes.

While the meat is baking, pass the sauce through a sieve, add the cream, and bring to the boil. Stir in the cornflour with the rest of the white wine, add salt and sugar to taste, plus the second half of the apple, sliced finely, and boil up briefly again.

Arrange the rabbit fillets on a dish with some of the sauce, serving the rest separately. Haricot beans make a good accompaniment, as do Spätzle or boiled potatoes; a well-cooled, elegant Kerner wine adds the final touch.

It is not all that long ago that one or two barrels of cider were to be found in the cellar of almost every Swabian house, and Papa drew off a stoneware jug or two of it in the evening. Now most of the old barrels have dried out and cracked, and many have suffered the indignity of being sawn in two halves to serve as flower tubs. Recent times, however, have seen a revival of interest in cider, and it is beginning to reassert itself as a desirable drink.

SADDLE OF VENISON WITH CELERIAC PURÉE

1 saddle of venison (roe-buck), approx. 2.2 kg (5 lb)
Seasoning: mixture of salt, black pepper, marjoram, thyme, rosemary, and coriander (see below)
3 tablespoons oil
250 ml (9 fl oz) Lemberger (red wine)
½ litre (¾ pint) venison stock (recipe on p. 100)
2 tablespoons port
1 teaspoon lemon juice
salt, freshly-milled pepper
1 tablespoon cranberries
20 g (1 oz) butter

The celeriac purée:
250 g (9 oz) celeriac
150 ml (5 fl oz) vegetable stock or water
3 tablespoons double cream
salt, freshly-milled pepper
nutmeg
2 tablespoons cream

NB:
The seasoning mixture used here is also good for other roasts. It keeps for some time in a jar out of the light. To make it, pound 10 g (⅓ oz) each of marjoram, thyme, and rosemary, and 5 g (⅙ oz) each of black pepper and coriander in a mortar, and mix with 100 g (4 oz) salt.

Preheat the oven to 200 °C (400 °F). Cut the fillet together with the rib-meat from the saddle, and remove all skin and tendons. Rub the meat with the seasoning mixture. Heat oil in a pan, and brown the rib meat on all sides. Then roast the whole for 8 minutes in the preheated oven. Take the meat out of the oven, wrap in aluminium foil, and allow to rest for a few minutes. The meat should still be pink in the middle. Then keep hot. Skim the fat off the gravy, heat, add the red wine, top up with the venison stock, and boil down somewhat. Add port, lemon juice, salt, pepper, and cranberries to taste. Pass the sauce through a fine sieve, and mix a few dabs of butter into it with the mixer.
Peel the celeriac, dice finely, and simmer in the vegetable stock or water till soft. Pour off the liquid, allow to stand for a while, then add the double cream and blend in the mixer. Return to the pot, reduce a little, season, and finally fold in the whisked cream.
Cut the pieces of saddle diagonally into slices, arrange on a dish, and pour a little of the sauce over them. Serve with pears cooked in red wine and hand-made Spätzle.

Select a fairly robust red wine to go with it – a Spätburgunder, or a Samtrot, perhaps, and serve it chambré: about 16 °C (60 °F), not the temperature of the room!

In my 100-year-old "Universal Encyclopaedia of the Art of Cooking" the section on "Saddle of Venison" begins: "The saddle is the most succulent and tender part of the deer, and a saddle of venison is considered to be one of the most excellent roasts, so that it is suited as a main course for any stylish dinner party." As our forests are now finally clear of the effects of the Chernobyl disaster, we can once again confidently include this "most excellent roast" in our more ambitious dinner menus.

VENISON KNUCKLES WITH CHERRY SAUCE

8 knuckles of venison
(roe-buck or doe)
flavouring vegetables, consisting of:
100 g (4 oz) onions,
50 g (2 oz) celeriac,
30 g (1 oz) leek
salt and pepper
2 litres (3½ pints) venison
stock (recipe on p. 100)
30 g (1 oz) tomato purée
200 ml (7 fl oz) red wine
6 juniper berries
2 cloves
1 bay leaf
50 g (2 oz) cranberry jelly
or cranberries
20 ml (1 fl oz) brandy
1 pinch of sugar
100 g (4 oz) fresh cher-
ries, stoned
2 tablespoons butter
20 ml (1 fl oz) Armagnac

NB:
*Depending on the season,
other fruits, such as
plums, hips, or quinces,
can be substituted for
cherries.*

Trim the knuckles, cutting the bone back as far as possible. Chop the vegetables roughly and stew for a while. Season the knuckles with salt and pepper, and fry brief-ly in very hot oil. Remove, and fry the bones, adding the venison stock in two or three phases, then put in the tomato purée and sim-mer briefly. Add the red wine and top up with venison stock. Bring the sauce to the boil, and add the venison and the pounded herbs. Braise for about 1½ hours. Remove the knuckles once the meat can be easily detached from the bone, and allow to cool.

Add the cranberry jelly and the brandy to the sauce, bring to the boil, and pass through a sieve. Reduce to half the quantity, then add salt and sugar to taste.

Fry the cherries gently in butter, add the Armagnac, and then pour in the sauce. Boil well again together with the meat, then free the meat from the bones.

Nut Spätzle make a good accompa-niment. To make these, mix the cooked Spätzle (recipe on p.134) with chopped walnuts and a little butter just before serving. The wine to go with this dish should be along the lines of those suggested for Saddle of Venison in the previous recipe.

*I*n culinary German, "Haxe" normally means the part of the leg below the haunch, and above or below the "knee". In England this is more or less the same as the shank end in mutton, or the knuckle or hand in pork, but the French cut "jambonneau" comes nearest to what the Germans understand by "Haxe".

CHRISTMAS GOOSE

1 oven-ready goose
(approx. 3–4 kg /
6¾ lb–9 lb)
salt and pepper
1 tablespoon chopped
mugwort
4 stoned prunes
1 apple
50 g (2 oz) sultanas
2 tablespoons bread-
crumbs
cinnamon, sugar
grated rind of ½ an
untreated lemon
1 onion
1 small carrot
½ leek
¼ celeriac
1 tablespoon tomato purée

1 litre (1¾ pints) water or
broth
salt, pepper

NB:
*A fresh goose is far superior
to a deep-frozen one.
The goose fat from roast-
ing can be made into an
excellent sandwich spread:
mix with half the quantity
of lard so that it spreads
better, and add some lightly
fried diced onion and
apple.*

Preheat the oven to 180 °C
(350 °F). Cut out the larger fat
deposits, keep the neck and
giblets in the fridge for one of the
next few days. Wash the goose
inside and out thoroughly, dry,
rub with salt, pepper, and mugwort, and prick the skin in a
number of places.
Mix the prunes, sliced apple, and
sultanas with the breadcrumbs,
flavour to taste with cinnamon,
sugar, and grated lemon rind, and
stuff the goose with the mixture.
Sew the goose shut and fry briefly
in the roasting pan with the
breast downwards. Add some
water, and roast in the preheated
oven for about 3 hours. After half
the roasting time turn the goose
onto its back, and add some
more water. Skim off the fat from
the gravy. During the last half
an hour baste several times with
cold water so that the skin
crispens.
When it is cooked, take the goose
out of the pan and keep hot.
Briefly boil up the finely chopped
vegetables with the tomato purée
in the gravy, and add water,
repeating this process three
times. Then top up with water or
broth, season to taste with salt
and pepper, and simmer for a
while. Sieve the sauce. Before
serving, cut the threads with
which the goose is sewn up,
remove the stuffing with a large
spoon, and arrange on a dish.
Serve with potato dumplings and
red cabbage cooked with apples.

*M*ugwort *is also aptly called
"goose herb" in German,
but it could equally well be called
duck, sheep, or pig herb, for it
not only tastes good with all
these fatty roasts, but also make
them more easily digestible.
Mugwort likes calcareous soil,
and will flourish in any sunny,
well-drained spot in your garden,
but is also to be found growing
wild on wasteland and waysides.
Cut complete leaf-stalks off in
July or August before the flowers
open. Remove the leaves, and
hang up to dry with only the
buds. Keep without the stalks in
an air-tight jar away from the
light.*

Pasta, Potato, and Vegetable Dishes

ALLGÄU CHEESE SPÄTZLE
LIVER SPÄTZLE

ALLGÄU CHEESE SPÄTZLE
Basic Spätzle recipe:
450 g (1 lb) plain flour
6 eggs
salt

The cheese Spätzle:
200 g (½ lb) Allgäu "Berg-käse" (Gruyère will do), or Emmenthal
freshly-ground pepper
125 ml (4½ fl oz) cream
2 onions
80 g (3 oz) butter
1 tablespoon whipped cream
4 tablespoons chives

LIVER SPÄTZLE:
For the Spätzle batter:
250 g (9 oz) plain flour
250 g (9 oz) oxliver
2 eggs
1 onion
1 teaspoon marjoram
nutmeg
salt, fresh-milled pepper

For the crust:
60 g (2 oz) butter, 6 eggs

NB:
The flour should not be too fine, because coarser flour gives the "Spätzle" more bite. If you prefer a lighter version of the Cheese Spätzle, substitute broth for the cream.

ALLGÄU CHEESE SPÄTZLE
Preheat the oven to 180 °C (350 °F). Beat – the longer the better – the flour and eggs, with salt and a little water, into a smooth dough then allow to rest for 10–20 minutes. Put some of the dough on a wet board, and scrape slivers of dough off it with a slice straight into boiling salted water (alternatively force the batter through a potato press). Allow to boil until the Spätzle float on the surface. Take out with a slotted spoon, and, if the Spätzle are intended only as a side dish, allow them to drain briefly on a cake rack, then transfer to a dish. For the cheese Spätzle, remove them from the boiling water, as above; put them in an oven-proof dish in layers, alternating with the freshly grated cheese, peppering each layer. Then pour the cream over the whole. Bake in the preheated oven for approx. 15 minutes until the cheese melts.
Peel and slice the onions, and fry till golden-brown in the butter. Pour over the Spätzle together with the whipped cream, and bake again briefly. Sprinkle with chives just before serving.
To make up a complete meal, serve with the Spätzle either a

mixed salad or grated potato salad (recipe on p. 58).

LIVER SPÄTZLE
Mix the flour, the finely-minced liver, and the eggs to form a dough. Chop the onions finely, blanch, and add to the mixture. Season the dough, and beat well. Allow to rest for 10–15 minutes, then scrape into boiling water, as described above.
Lightly fry the finished Liver Spätzle in butter, break the eggs over them, and slowly cook till the eggs set. Arrange like a pancake on a flat dish. As side dishes, serve endive salad, or grated potato salad (recipe on p. 58) mixed with thin slices of cucumber.

LENTILS AND SPÄTZLE

500 g (1 lb) lentils
1 onion
1 bay leaf
1 clove
1 tablespoon lard
1 tablespoon plain flour
1 teaspoon tomato purée
1 teaspoon grated horse-radish
1/2 teaspoon medium-hot mustard
1 tablespoon white wine vinegar
salt, pepper

Meat, sausages, and garnish:
1 smoked fillet of pork
4 smoked chaps of pork
1 carrot
1/2 celeriac
4 pork sausages
1 tablespoon lard
1 small sprig of parsley

NB:
The lentils need a dash of vinegar, but only add it when they are soft; the acidity otherwise prevents them from softening.

Wash the lentils and put them in salted water. Stick one half of the onion with the bay leaf and clove, and simmer with the lentils for about 1 hour.

In the meantime, cut the second half of the onion in small dice, and fry in a pan together with the lard and flour to form a brown roux. Allow this to get cold.

At the end of the cooking period, take the stuck onion out of the lentils, add the tomato purée, boil up briefly, and stir in the roux. Flavour to taste with horseradish, mustard, vinegar, salt, and pepper. Now prepare the Spätzle according to the basic recipe on the previous page, and keep hot in a closed dish.

Put the fillet and chaps of pork in lightly salted boiling water, and allow to simmer very gently for about 1 1/2 hours till tender. After half of the cooking period add the peeled carrot and celeriac.

Fry the sausages well all round in lard. Put the lentils in a dish, slice the fillet and chaps, and arrange on top of the lentils with the sausages. Garnish with thin slices of carrot and celeriac and chopped parsley.

For some people, the word "lentils" calls to mind Jacob and Esau and the "bread and pottage of lentiles", and how they bargained about Esau's birthright. But we Swabians first think of ourselves, and follow up "Lentils", with "and Spätzle, and . . ." What we substitute for the three dots depends on our present mood. If we are feeling modest, then it will be a simple kind of sausage, if not, then it will probably be something along the lines of the additions given in our recipe. In any case it will make a substantial, tasty meal and what could go better with it than a beer, or better still, and more traditional, a well-made cider?

TWO KINDS
OF ROLLED NOODLES

BUBESPITZLE
500 g (generous 1 lb)
potatoes, boiled the pre-
vious day
125 g (4½ oz) plain flour
1 egg
salt, nutmeg
lard for frying

SPINDELE
Potatoes, flour, egg,
salt, and nutmeg, as above
1 small onion
30 g (1 oz) fat bacon
1 tablespoon finely chopped
parsley
50 g (2 oz) beans
60 g (2 oz) butter

BUBESPITZLE (above)
Grate the boiled potatoes, and
knead into a dough together with
the flour and egg; flavour with
salt and nutmeg. From this dough
form small, pointed sausages with
the hands, and cook for 2 minutes in salted water. Remove with
a slotted spoon, dry briefly on
kitchen paper, and then fry
golden-brown in plenty of lard.

SPINDELE (below)
Cut the onion and bacon into
small dice, fry briefly, then mix
together with the finely chopped
parsley and the potato, flour and
egg mixture described above.
Cook the beans briefly in boiling
water, so that they are still firm,
and then shape the mixture
round the individual beans to
form the Spindele. Fry in butter.

*In Swabian "Bubespitzle"
acquired their name because of
their shape, which is undoubtedly
reminiscent of that certain part
of a small boy's anatomy (Bube =
boy) that differentiates it from a
small girl's. But the Swabians are
a broad-minded folk, and its
name in no way lessens their
appetite for this dish – and
rightly, too, because it can be
quite delicious!*
*The basic recipe can be varied
slightly – for example, by dipping
the cooked "Bubespitzle" in
reduced cream, or mixing them
with sauerkraut.*
*The Italians use a very similar
mixture to make splendid
"gnocchi di patate", which are
given their special character by
the addition of fresh herbs, such
as basil, or of spinach. As will be
seen from the recipe, "Spindele"
are really just a variation of
"Bubespitzle" with a core of
haricot beans.*

NOODLES

BASIC RECIPE FOR
NOODLE DOUGH:
300 g (10 ½ oz) plain flour
2 eggs, 1 egg yolk
½ tablespoon oil, salt

SPINACH NOODLES
The spinach concentrate:
130 g (5 oz) spinach
2 tablespoons water
noodle ingredients as in
the basic recipe above

MUSHROOM NOODLES
The concentrate:
250 g (9 oz) fresh or deep-
frozen boletus mushrooms
1 tablespoon fat
salt, pepper, nutmeg

The noodle dough:
300 g (10 ½ oz) plain flour
2 egg yolks, 1 egg
½ tablespoon olive oil

NB:
*The dough becomes more
pliable if you leave it to
rest for a while after
kneading.
Home-made noodles
should be used as fresh as
possible. They will keep
for 1–2 days when dried.*

BASIC NOODLE DOUGH:
Heap the flour on a pastry board,
and make a well in the middle.
Whisk the eggs and egg yolk with
oil and salt, and pour the mixture
into the well. Gradually mix the
flour into the liquid, working
inwards from the outside, and
knead the whole into a smooth
dough; form into a ball, wrap in
foil, and allow to rest in a cool
place for 2 hours. (If you use a
blender, add the ingredients one
by one to the flour, mixing slowly
at first, then faster.)
Roll the dough out as thinly as
possible into rectangular pieces,
and cut into strips about ½ cm
wide. Allow to dry a little before
cooking.
If the noodles are not needed
straight away dry them thoroughly, and keep in airtight jars.

SPINACH NOODLES
To make the concentrate, remove
the stalks from the spinach, and
wash the leaves thoroughly.
Purée the leaves with 2 tablespoons of water in the blender,
and pass through a cloth. Boil up
the resulting liquid, stirring all
the time, salt, and then strain
through a strong paper napkin.
The resulting concentrate left on
the napkin is mixed with the

eggs, and the noodles made as
described above.

MUSHROOM NOODLES
Fresh boletus mushrooms should
be trimmed and thoroughly
washed under running cold
water; deep-frozen ones should be
slightly thawed. Fry very lightly
in a flat pan with a little hot fat,
and season with salt, pepper, and
nutmeg. Purée the cooled mushrooms in the blender, and make a
concentrate of them, as explained
in the Spinach Noodle recipe.
Make the noodles as described
above.

*N*oodles are coloured with
aromatics such as spinach,
tomatoes, beetroot, or saffron. So
first a concentrate is prepared
to provide the required colour.
Please note that, in contrast to
Italian pasta, which is cooked al
dente, Swabian noodles contain
no Durum wheat, so that they
become somewhat softer when
cooked.
Noodles taste particularly good in
combination with mushrooms.*

SCHWABENHANSEL CREAM NOODLES

100 g (4 oz) boiled ham
1 onion
½ cucumber
60 g (2 oz) mushrooms
80 g (3 oz) butter
salt, freshly-ground pepper
3 tablespoons crème
fraîche
600 g (1½ lb) noodles
2 small tomatoes
small bunches of chervil,
parsley, and tarragon
nutmeg

Cut the ham, onion, cucumber, and mushrooms in thin slices. Heat the butter in a pan, sautée the ham and onion briefly, add the cucumber and mushrooms, and season with pepper and salt. Put in the crème fraîche.

Drain the freshly cooked noodles, and mix them with the diced tomatoes and the finely chopped herbs. Add a pinch of salt and nutmeg to taste.

This is a simple dish which can equally well be accompanied by Swabian potato salad (recipe on p. 58) or a mixed salad; try using cider vinegar for a change for the salad dressing. Swabians often top the cream noodles with a fried egg.

Wild mushrooms are more aromatic than the farmed kind, but if you go mushroom-hunting yourself, it is advisable, to say the least, to be able to distinguish between edible and poisonous varieties. The common edible mushrooms, such as the field or horse mushroom can be used for this dish, but the variety we call "Stone Mushroom" in Swabia is even tastier, and has firmer flesh. It grows in groups along stony waysides, and as its specific Latin name, bitorquis, indicates, it has two rings on its stem instead of the usual one.

SWABIAN RAVIOLI

Not quite in line with our recipe, as what is shown here is intended for only four to five persons, but captured at the decisive moment: just as the stuffing is being covered.

For 10 persons
The noodle dough:
750 g (just under 1¾ lb) plain flour
6 eggs, salt
6 tablespoons water

The stuffing:
2 bread rolls
50 g (2 oz) leek
250 g (9 oz) spinach
50 g (2 oz) streaky bacon
1 onion
500 g (1 lb) mincemeat
500 g (1 lb) veal sausage meat
4 eggs, salt and pepper
nutmeg, marjoram
1 egg yolk

Roll out the finished dough very thin, and cut in strips about 100x20cm.

For the stuffing, squeeze the rolls which have been soaked in water, and put them through the mincer together with the blanched leek and spinach. Briefly fry the diced bacon, chop the onions finely and mix with the mince-meat, veal sausage meat, eggs, and puréed vegetables. Season to taste.

Brush one of the strips of dough with egg yolk, and arrange along one of its edges a roughly 5cm-thick sausage of the stuffing. Roll into a cylinder, press it slightly flat, and then cut into about 7cm-long rhombus-shaped pieces. Press the dough together at the ends of each section to close them. Repeat this process for the rest of the dough and stuffing, and cook the "ravioli" for about 15 minutes in boiling salted water until they are done.

Maultaschen can be eaten simply boiled; or boiled and buttered; or boiled, sliced, and lightly fried (if wished, with a beaten egg over them). When buttered or fried, they are best accompanied by potato salad (recipe on p. 58).

*T*he true Swabian does not worry about the origins of "Maultaschen", is not concerned about whether they were invented in China or elswhere: good things are always invented at least twice! The basic question is: should they contain spinach or not? This is a problem that has broken up marriages and shat-tered whole families. We believe that spinach is an essential ingre-dient, as necessary as the Amen in church! But if you prefer them without spinach, do please your-self!

And here is another tip related to this inexhaustible subject: "Maul-taschen" can be used to make a tasty, sustaining salad: cut the warm "Maultaschen" in slices and toss in a dressing of wine vinegar, oil, salt, sugar, and finely-chopped chives and the stalks of spring onions. Season to taste with salt and fresh-milled pepper, serve on lettuce leaves, and garnish with a radish. Plan four "Maultaschen" per person.

GAISBURG STEW

4 marrow bones
600 g (1 1/2 lb) beef
(brisket)
1 1/2–2 litres
(2 1/2–3 1/2 pints) water
1 tablespoon salt
2 carrots
1/4 celeriac
1 parsley root
1/2 leek
1 bay leaf
4 peppercorns
2 juniper berries
4–5 potatoes
salt, pepper, nutmeg
about 250 g (9 oz) Spätzle
(recipe on p. 134)

The garnish:
1 onion
50 g (2 oz) butter
2 tablespoons chopped
chives

Wash the marrow bones well in hot water, put into a pot with cold water and rapidly bring to the boil. Add the meat, salt, and simmer slowly for about 2 hours. After 1 1/2 hours put in the finely-chopped vegetables, the bay leaf, peppercorns, and juniper berries. Peel and slice the potatoes.
Take the meat out and keep it hot. Sieve the liquid, return the vegetables to it, and simmer gently. Boil the potatoes quickly till soft, drain, and add to the liquid. In the meantime prepare the Spätzle. Cut the meat in cubes, put it back in the liquid together with the Spätzle, and boil up again briefly. Flavour with nutmeg, salt, and pepper.
For the garnish, peel and slice the onions, fry them briefly in butter till golden, and, before serving, scatter them on top of the stew together with the chives.

We Swabians agree on at least one thing: a good "Gaisburger Marsch" is well worth eating! What we do not agree on is the origin of the name. Was it invented by a Gaisburg innkeeper, who combined all the available leftovers to make a sustaining meal for soldiers marching off to war? Or was it the traditional dish taken by the wives of ne'er-do-wells locked up in the Gaisburg jail, which, of course, had to be something both tasty and nourishing; this seems less likely, as the inmates were certainly not allowed to march anywhere, except, presumably, in some cases, to the gallows.
Only one thing is certain: Gaisburg, which gives it name to this truly Swabian dish, and which was once a village outside Stuttgart, is now one of that city's most delightful quarters.

Yeast Dumpling with Onion Garnish

300 g (¾ lb) plain flour
15 g (½ oz) yeast
¼ litre (9 fl oz) lukewarm milk
1 egg
salt
60 g (2 oz) white bread without crust
1 onion
2 tablespoons parsley
1 tablespoon chervil
1 tablespoon chives
30 g (1 oz) butter
pepper, nutmeg

The garnish:
50 g (2 oz) butter
1 onion
2–3 teaspoons bread-crumbs

NB:
If you want to serve yeast dumplings as a main course, mix 150 g (5 oz) of diced ham into the dough.

Heap the flour in a bowl, make a well in the centre, crumble the yeast into it, add the milk, the beaten egg, and a pinch of salt, and knead into a dough. Cover up, and put in a warm place to rise.

In the meantime, cut the white bread and onions into small dice, and chop the herbs. Fry the diced white bread and onion gently in butter, and allow to get cold. When the yeast dough has risen to twice its original size, knead in the mixture of white bread, onion, herbs, and season to taste; roll in a floured cloth, and tie up the two ends of the cloth. Poach in boiling water for about an hour till done. Unwrap the dumpling, cut in slices, and garnish with the onion and breadcrumbs fried golden-brown in butter.

Whether you serve the dumpling as a side-dish with a roast, or as a main course with diced ham, as described above, it is a good idea also to provide a salad, or a summer vegetable such as haricot beans – for optical as well as health reasons.

The wide variety of dumplings that form a characteristic part of the German cuisine also boast a wide variety of names, depending on the part of the German-speaking world in which you eat them: "Klösse", "Knödel", "Knopf", or "Knöpfle", "Klops", "Knockerl". They are not always a culinary delight – but they certainly can be if they are made properly so that they form a light and fluffy alternative to potatoes.

LIVER DUMPLINGS
BACON DUMPLINGS

LIVER DUMPLINGS
6–7 day-old bread rolls
125 ml (4½ fl oz) milk
1 onion
50 g (2 oz) bacon
2 tablespoons chopped
parsley
30 g (1 oz) butter
500 g (18 oz) oxliver
2 eggs
salt, marjoram, freshly-
milled pepper
1 litre (1¾ pints) good
meat broth

BACON DUMPLINGS
7 day-old bread rolls
125 ml (4½ fl oz) milk
3 eggs
salt, pepper
80 g (3 oz) streaky bacon
1 small onion
2 tablespoons chopped
parsley
30 g (1 oz) butter

NB:
*If the dough is too thin
(bread rolls are not the
same size everywhere!),
you can mix in about
1 tablespoon plain flour as
required. Do not over-salt
the bacon dumplings.*

LIVER DUMPLINGS (below)
Cut the rolls into small pieces, and soak in lukewarm milk. Finely dice the onion and bacon, briefly fry in butter with the parsley, and allow to cool. Mince the liver finely, add the rolls after squeezing surplus milk out of them, and mix in the onion, bacon, parsley, and eggs. Season well. Scoop dumplings out of the mixture with a tablespoon, put into the seething broth, and allow to simmer gently for about 20 minutes till done.
Liver Dumplings are equally good whether served directly in the broth, or, garnished, as a main dish. If served as a main course, they can be accompanied by potato salad mixed with endives to provide a contrast of colour and taste. Sauerkraut is an equally suitable side-dish. Some Swabians like to go the whole way and have a dish of Spätzle on the side, too.

BACON DUMPLINGS (above)
Cut the rolls into small pieces, and soak in lukewarm milk. Mix the eggs together with the salt and pepper, pour over the rolls, and allow to steep for ½ hour. In the meantime, dice the bacon and onion finely, and sautée briefly with the parsley. Then combine with the dough, and, with wet hands, form small round dumplings. Poach in seething water for about 15 minutes till done.

T he German cuisine is not the only one to feature dumplings. Both English and French (Alsatian) cookery provide some interesting variations on the theme, some of them sweet, like the English apple dumplings, and some tiny, like the Alsatian "noques".

BREAD SOUFFLÉ WITH MUSHROOMS

3 bread rolls
½ onion
20 g (1 oz) fat bacon
1 tablespoon chopped chives
1 tablespoon chopped parsley
30 g (1 oz) butter
1 egg yolk
125 ml (4½ fl oz) cream
salt, nutmeg
2 egg whites

The mushrooms:
500 g (generous 1 lb) boletus mushrooms
1 small onion
30 g (1 oz) butter
salt, freshly-milled pepper
nutmeg
⅛ litre (4½ fl oz) cream
1 small bunch parsley
chervil as decoration

NB:
Mushrooms should if possible be used on the day on which they are picked or bought. If they have to be kept overnight, spread them out in a cool, airy place.
Sautée the mushrooms in an open pot, otherwise they become hard. Never reheat mushrooms!

Preheat the oven to 180 °C (350 °F). Cut the rolls into small dice. Chop the onion and bacon, lightly sautée them in butter together with the chopped herbs, then add the diced rolls, egg yolk, and cream. Flavour to taste with nutmeg and salt. Fold the stiffly beaten egg whites into the mixture, and fill it into buttered cassolettes (individual casseroles). Put the cassolettes into a bain-marie with hot water, and bake in the preheated oven.

Trim the mushrooms thoroughly with a knife, removing any soft, or suspect parts, and the hard parts of the stem. Wash, and cut into even slices. Fry the diced onion briefly in butter; add the mushrooms, sautée briefly, and season with salt, pepper, and nutmeg. Pour the cream onto the mushrooms, and sprinkle the freshly-chopped parsley over them.

To serve, turn the soufflés out on plates, add the mushrooms, and garnish with the chervil.

This delicate, light meal is best complemented by an equally light rosé, or a Schillerwein.

Tradition and progress could be the motto to go with this recipe, which is a modern version of the good old-fashioned bread dumplings. In the way of individual casseroles Grand-mother would probably only have had the kind shown in the illustration on p. 173, and the idea of the bain-marie would also have been foreign to her.

HERB STRUDEL

up with the help of the cloth, and place on a buttered baking tin. Brush the strudel with butter and bake in the preheated oven for about 45 minutes.

Strudel are always served hot. Together with a tomato sauce, the herb strudel makes a wonderfully light non-meat dish.

When Count Eberhard the Bearded of Württemberg, the founder of Tübingen University, brought his bride Barbara home from Mantua in 1474, there was a great wedding feast with 22 courses for those of princely rank. Noble ladies and gentlemen of lesser rank had to make do with 12 courses, and the servants with 6. The fifteenth course of the princely menu, preceded by "Baked trout", and followed by "A brown purée", was "Wafers, filled, and baked" – and this was in all likelihood what we now call "Strudel".

The dough:
125 g (4½ oz) plain flour
1 pinch salt
50 ml (1¾ fl oz) water
1 tablespoon olive oil
The filling:
a small bunch each of
parsley and chervil
2 tablespoons chopped
chives, 1 onion
130 g (5 oz) butter
50 g (2 oz) breadcrumbs
2 egg yolks
100 g (4 oz) sour cream
salt, pepper, nutmeg
butter for the baking tin
and for brushing the strudel

NB:
Put the cloth on which you intend to stretch the dough on a warm baking sheet. The warmth makes the dough more pliable.

Preheat the oven to 180°C (350 °F). Mix the ingredients for the dough in a basin, and knead well on a floured surface. Wrap the dough in foil, and allow it to rest in a warm place.

Chop the herbs finely for the filling. Dice the onion, and fry gently in a third of the butter; add the breadcrumbs, fry a little further, then allow to cool. Cream the rest of the butter, add the egg yolk bit by bit, then fold in the sour cream. Add the cooled bread-crumbs and the herbs to the butter mix, and season to taste.

Take the dough out of the foil, roll it out, and then stretch it thin on a floured cloth. Spread the filling on the dough, roll the whole

SOUR POTATO WHEELS

1 kg (2¼ lb) potatoes
1 onion
50 g (2 oz) lard
2 tablespoons plain flour
½ litre (¾ pint) cold broth
spices: 4 crushed peppercorns, 1 bay leaf, 1 clove, salt, nutmeg, freshly-milled pepper
medium-hot mustard
2 tablespoons cider vinegar

NB:
Either mix cold broth into warm roux, or cold roux into warm broth – otherwise lumps are formed. Tea eggs, mostly of silver, are not very popular because the tea cannot develop its full aroma in them. But they are useful, as here, as "spice eggs", for unground spices, as they are easy to retrieve when they have served their purpose.

Cook and peel the potatoes. Fry the onions lightly in lard, then dust with flour, and fry golden-brown. Top up with broth, add the spice egg, then the other ingredients to taste, and simmer for a while. Take the spice egg out. Cut the potatoes in slices ("wheels"), put them in the liquor, and boil up again briefly. Boiled brisket of beef or calf's tongue cooked with a slice of celeriac, a parsley root, and a carrot goes extremely well with this dish. But do not forget to serve a salad, too.

Every Swabian should know what is meant by "Saure Rädle", but although this was at one time a "national dish", it has unfortunately gone out of fashion a bit, like Gaisburg Stew. So we have to add "potato" to the name to make sure it is universally understood, although the word potato is itself alien, as the Swabians have at least four other dialect words for it – two of which translate into English as "earth pears", or "ground apples".

SAUERKRAUT

or game birds. In winter it is a valuable source of vitamins (B1 and C).

Although sauerkraut is generally regarded as the German dish, it is also popular in many other countries, such as France, especially the Alsace, a number of East European countries, and in parts of the United States. The indigestibility sometimes attributed to sauerkraut normally derives from the salted, smoked, or fatty meats and sausage which are often served with it. Sauerkraut can be further refined by the addition of pieces of pineapple or peeled grapes. When served with game birds a dash of champagne or dry sparkling wine adds zest.

1 onion
3 tablespoons lard
1 kg (2¼ lb) sauerkraut
250 ml (9 fl oz) Riesling or cider
125 ml (4½ fl oz) water
muslin bag of spices containing 3 bay leaves,
1 clove of garlic, 1 clove,
2 juniper berries, thyme
4 tablespoons apple purée
1 potato
pepper, salt if necessary

NB:
Do not wash the sauerkraut before cooking, as this robs it of its flavour and a number of valuable elements. Be sparing with salt.

Chop the onion small, and fry briefly in a large pot in hot lard. Loosen the sauerkraut, add to the onion, and fry further for a bit. Add the wine or cider and the water, and put in the bag of spices. Cook on a low flame for about 2 hours. If you use canned sauerkraut the cooking time is only about half an hour. Just before the end of the cooking period, remove the spice bag, add the apple purée, and stir in the raw, grated potato. Season with pepper, and possibly add a little more Riesling or cider to taste.

Sauerkraut is the right – and sometimes the only acceptable – side-dish to serve with strong-flavoured food such as fried liver,

Sauerkraut Soufflé Savoury Cakes

SAUERKRAUT SOUFFLÉ
1 small onion
50 g (2 oz) white bread
without crust
250 ml (9 fl oz) cream
75 g (3 oz) butter
125 ml (4½ fl oz) white
wine
300 g (11 oz) sauerkraut
2 egg yolks
1 egg white
salt, pepper, sugar

SAVOURY CAKES
½ onion
30 g (1 oz) butter
125 g (4 ½ oz) sauerkraut
2 tablespoons pearl barley
4 tablespoons white wine
500 g (generous 1 lb) raw
potatoes
2 eggs
100 g (4 oz) white bread
without crust
salt, freshly-milled pepper
nutmeg
100 g (4 oz) clarified butter

SAUERKRAUT SOUFFLÉ
Preheat oven to 170 °C (325 °F).
Chop the onion and dice the
white bread small; reduce the
cream to half quantity.
Fry the chopped onion in a third
of the butter without browning,
pour on the white wine, and
reduce it to almost nothing.
Loosen the sauerkraut, and add it
to the onions. Gently fry the
diced bread in the rest of the
butter, add to the sauerkraut
together with the reduced cream,
and allow to get cold. Stir in the
egg yolks, and fold in the stiffly
beaten egg white. Taste for seasoning, then fill into cassolettes,
and bake in the preheated oven
for about 30 minutes. Turn out,
and serve.

SAVOURY CAKES
Brown the finely chopped onions
lightly in the butter. Cook the
sauerkraut and pearl barley in the
white wine. Add the fried chopped
onion, and allow the mixture to
cool.
In the meantime grate the peeled
raw potatoes, and then mix with
the cooled sauerkraut. Add the
eggs and the crumbled white
bread, and season. Shape the
mixture into flat cakes, and fry
golden-brown in clarified butter.

These savoury cakes go best with
rich meat dishes such as roast
sucking pig or roast hock of pork,
and a glass of beer.

*I*f you have a cool cellar it is
worthwhile making your own
sauerkraut, for which you need a
large stoneware crock. You will
be amazed at how good it tastes.
Clean the cabbage, and slice finely. Place in layers in the crock,
pressing down each layer firmly
with your fist; salt each layer. The
crock should be firmly closed so
that it ferments properly – either
with a well-fitting wooden lid, or
with a plastic sack filled with
water. The lactic acid bacteria
develop best at room temperature. After two days, put the
crock in the cellar. The sauerkraut will be ready to eat two to
four weeks later. If the sauerkraut
is kept for a longer period in the
stoneware crock, the lid should
be washed at regular intervals.*

AUTUMN STEW

2 onions
3 tablespoons oil
600 g (1 1/2 lb) brisket of
beef
salt
1 1/2 litres (2 1/2 pints)
water
1 leek
1/2 celeriac
200 g (7 oz) carrots
1/2 savoy cabbage
300 g (3/4 lb) potatoes
spice bag with
1 bay leaf,
5 crushed peppercorns,
2 crushed cloves garlic,
2 juniper berries, and
1 clove
salt, freshly-milled pepper
nutmeg
1 small bunch chives

NB:
*Stews can be prepared in
many different ways. A
shoulder of lamb can be
used instead of the beef
given here, for example.
Stews warm up well.*

Slice the onions finely, and fry in hot oil without browning. Cut the meat in cubes, add it to the onions, and fry for a further ten minutes.
Salt, fill up with water, and simmer for about 80 minutes. Wash the vegetables, cut the leek in thin strips. Peel the celeriac and carrots, dice them, and add to the stew. Remove the stem from the savoy cabbage, chop the cabbage, and add to the stew together with the spice bag. About 1/2 hour later put in the potatoes and the leek. Simmer until the meat is tender. By then the stew will have thickened; season to taste with the salt, pepper, and nutmeg.
Serve garnished with freshly chopped chives.

A stew is not exactly ideal for a festive meal, but with all its good ingredients it makes a satisfying and nourishing dish. Stews are unfortunately often regarded as penny-pinching food, but they can be just right on a cold autumn or winter day.

FRIED VEGETARIAN SAUSAGE

a tomato and basil sauce. A healthy meal calls for a healthy drink – how about a glass of milk?

The small picture shows a Thanksgiving offering of the kind typical of the Fildern district.

150 g (5 oz) broccoli
150 g (5 oz) carrots
150 g (5 oz) haricot beans
200 g (just under ½ lb) cauli-flower
2 slices of lemon
200 ml (7 fl oz) cream
4 eggs, salt, freshly-milled pepper, nutmeg
1 sausage skin (from the butcher)

For coating:
60 g (2 oz) plain flour,
2 eggs
50 g (2 oz) parmesan

Fat for frying

NB:
Do not tie the sausage skin too tightly, as the filling expands somewhat while cooking.

Clean and wash the vegetables. Cut the broccoli into little rosettes, and blanch; peel the carrots, dice small, and blanch with the beans. Boil the cauliflower in salted water together with the lemon slices until it is soft, then cool (not in cold water!), and purée with the cream and eggs in the blender.

Mix the purée with the prepared vegetables, taste for seasoning, and fill the sausage skin with it. Boil in water for about an hour. Take the sausage out. Slice when it is cold. First coat the slices in flour, then in the egg-parmesan mixture; fry in hot fat.

Suitable side-dishes for this vegetarian sausage are spaghetti or noodles (recipe on p. 140), with

DESSERTS, CAKES, AND PASTRIES

COLD APPLE SOUP
SOUR MILK DELIGHT

COLD APPLE SOUP
450 g (1 lb) apples
20 g (1 oz) butter
sugar
125 ml (4½ fl oz) Riesling
or cider
250 ml (9 fl oz) apple juice
250 ml (9 fl oz) water
spice bag with:
¼ cinnamon stick
1 bay leaf, and 1 clove
½ lemon
horseradish

SOUR MILK DELIGHT
1/2 litre (1 pint) sour milk
500 g (1 lb) yoghurt
grated rind and juice of
1 untreated lemon
120 g (generous 4 oz)
icing sugar
20 g (1 oz) vanilla sugar

Fruits of the season:
apple or orange slices,
bananas, strawberries, or
raspberries

Garnish:
lemon melisse and chopped
hazelnuts

COLD APPLE SOUP
Wash and core the apples. Reserve one, slice the others, and fry gently in butter. Add a little sugar, then the white wine or cider, and reduce somewhat. Top up with apple juice and water, add the spice bag, and simmer for about ½ hour. Take off the flame, remove the spice bag, and purée the soup in the blender. Flavour to taste with a little sugar, lemon, and freshly-grated horseradish. Add the remaining apple, sliced thinly. Refrigerate and serve cold.

SOUR MILK DELIGHT
Put the ingredients except for the fruit and garnish in a bowl, and mix well in the blender. Put the prepared fruits in a bowl, pour the liquid over them, and refrigerate. Serve garnished with lemon melisse and chopped hazelnuts.

At some seasons the amount of fruit available – whether from one's own garden or the market – is so ample that the family's "minister of food" may well be glad of any suggestion as to how to serve it in attractive and varied ways, especially if the standard methods of using fruit – pies and fruits tarts, for example – have already been exhausted. The two very different suggestions on this page can either start or finish a meal. If served as a dessert, the apple soup should be sweetened rather more than given here, and the sour milk delight, if served as a starter, ra-ther less.

RHUBARB WITH STRAWBERRIES

RHUBARB CREAM WITH STRAWBERRIES

3 packets (or 18 leaves) of gelatine
350 g (¾ lb) fresh strawberries
200 g (just under ½ lb) rhubarb
80 g (3 oz) sugar
100 ml (4 fl oz) white wine, 2 egg whites
60 ml (2 fl oz) cream
Grand Marnier, lemon juice
icing sugar

STRAWBERRY AND RHUBARB JAM

500 g (1 lb) rhubarb
1 kg (2¼ lb) jam sugar containing pectin (if unavailable, see below)
500 g (1 lb) strawberries

NB:
Rhubarb is one of the best fresh products from our garden in early spring. But only the young stalks taste good. This tart "vegetable" combines extremely well with sweet strawberries. Absolute cleanliness is called for when jam making: the jars should be washed in very hot water or in the dish-washer! An interesting rhubarb jam varia-tion: 1 kg of rhubarb and 5–6 pieces of candied ginger cut very small. Here, too, you need 1 kg jam sugar with pectin.

RHUBARB CREAM WITH STRAWBERRIES

Soak the gelatine in cold water. Wash the strawberries and remove leaves and stalks. Wash the rhubarb, peel if necessary, cut in chunks, and cook till soft with 60 g (2 oz) sugar, 50 g (2 oz) strawberries, and the white wine. Then blend briefly, and pass through a fine sieve.

Squeeze out the soaked gelatine, add it to the still warm rhubarb purée, mix well, and refrigerate. Beat the egg white with the rest of the sugar till stiff; beat the cream separately till stiff. Fold the egg white into the cold fruit purée first, then the whisked cream. Finally add Grand Marnier and lemon juice to taste, and refrigerate. Garnish with strawberries cuts in various shapes and sprinkle with a little icing sugar.

STRAWBERRY AND RHUBARB JAM

Wash and peel the rhubarb, and cut into about 5mm (⅕ inch) slices. Put into a large pot in layers, sprinkling each layer with jam sugar containing pectin, and allow to steep and soften for at least 12 hours. Wash and drain the strawberries, remove the stalks, cut into pieces, and mix with the rhubarb. Bring the mixture to the boil, and boil fast for about 4 minutes; skim. Place the washed jars on a damp cloth, so that they do not crack, fill them to the brim with a ladle, screw on twist-off lids, and stand the jars upside down for about 5 minutes. This forms a hermetic seal.

If you prefer the old-fashioned method: have rubber rings and cellophane ready. Do not fill the jars quite so full, allow them to cool slightly, place a piece of cellophane cut to size and soaked in a saucer full of high-percentage rum or other alcohol on the surface of the jam. Cover the jar with cellophane and tie down or secure with a rubber band.

If jam sugar containing pectin is unavailable, use a separate jelling agent and follow the instructions on the packet.

CUP CAKES
PEACHES WITH SABAYON

CUP CAKES
4 egg yolks
50 g (2 oz) sugar
pinch of salt
1/2 litre (1 pint) milk
250 g (9 oz) flour
4 egg whites
60 g (2 oz) melted butter
grated rind of 1 untreated
lemon
icing sugar

PEACHES WITH SABAYON
3 egg yolks
40 g (1½ oz) sugar
125 ml (4½ fl oz) white
wine
dash of sparkling wine
100 ml (4 fl oz) cream
4 peaches
4 mint leaves for garnishing
4 scoops of vanilla ice-
cream

NB:
*Small peaches with pale
flesh are more fragrant
than the large, over-bred
varieties.*

CUP CAKES
Cream the egg yolks and sugar in
the blender, add the salt and
milk, and then stir in the flour by
the spoonful; add the grated
lemon rind. Finally, fold in the
whisked egg whites and the
melted butter.
Half fill the cassolettes with the
dough, and put them in the cold
oven on the bottom shelf. Bake at
180 °C (350 °F) for 1 hour.
Serve warm, sprinkled with icing
sugar to taste. The cakes can be
served with the wine cream from
the next recipe, with custard, or
with a sauce of puréed fruit.

PEACHES WITH SABAYON
Mix the egg yolks, sugar, wine,
and sparkling wine, then heat
carefully while continuing to
whisk till it begins to thicken.
Cool it by putting the basin into
iced water. Whisk until cold. Fold
in the cream.
Dip the peaches in boiling water,
peel and slice them. Pour the
sabayon, or wine cream, on
dessert plates, and arrange the
peaches around it in a semi-
circle. Garnish with mint leaves
and serve with vanilla ice-cream.

*The traditional kind of fire-
proof earthenware dishes
shown in our illustration are now
rarely seen in kitchens – except,
perhaps, hanging on the wall as
decorations. The cups in such
dishes were usually considerably
larger than the individual ones
called cassolettes, made of fire-
proof porcelain, glass, or metal.*

STEAMED DUMPLINGS
APPLE CHARLOTTE

**STEAMED
DUMPLINGS**
20 g (²/₃ oz) yeast
200 ml (7 fl oz) milk
330 g (¾ lb) plain flour
sugar
pinch of salt
grated rind of 1 untreated
lemon
1 egg
2 egg yolks
60 g (2 oz) butter
250 ml (9 fl oz) cream

The apple purée:
4 apples
20 g (1 oz) butter
100 ml (4 fl oz) white
wine
70 g (2½ oz) sugar
cinnamon

APPLE CHARLOTTE
6 day-old bread rolls
250 ml (9 fl oz) milk
6 cooking apples
250 g (9 oz) sugar
cinnamon
5 eggs
½ litre (just under 1 pint)
cream
50 g (2 oz) butter

STEAMED DUMPLINGS (below)
Dissolve the yeast in half of the milk (lukewarm), and stir in a lit-tle flour. Dust this dough with some flour, and allow to rise. Then add 2 tablespoons sugar, salt, grated lemon rind, egg, egg yolks, and the rest of the milk. Knead the dough well. Melt the butter and work it into the dough. Form dumplings the size of an egg, put them in a buttered form, cover with a cloth, and allow to rise again. In the mean-time, preheat the oven to 170 °C (325 °F) , and prepare the apple purée as given below. When the dumplings have risen, sprinkle them with sugar, pour the cream round them, and bake in the pre-heated oven for about 30 minu-tes.
Apple purée goes very well with this sweet: peel and core the apples, and cut in thickish slices. Fry the slices briefly in the butter, and top up with the white wine; add the sugar and a pinch of cin-namon, and cook further. When the apple is soft, purée it in the blender or pass it through a sieve. The apple purée is served warm with the freshly-baked dumplings.

APPLE CHARLOTTE (above)
Preheat the oven to 160°C (300 °F). Slice the rolls, and soak in milk for a while. Peel and core the apples, and slice them thinly. Line a cake tin (or spring-form pan) with non-stick baking paper and put in a layer of the soaked rolls. Pile the apples on this, sprinkle with sugar and cinna-mon (about 50 g/2 oz), and cover with the rest of the rolls. Mix the remaining milk, the beaten eggs, 200 g (9 oz) sugar, and the cream together, and pour into the cake tin. Put dabs of butter on the top, and bake in the preheated oven for 1½ hours. After 1 hour, cover the tin with aluminiun foil.
Turn the charlotte out onto a flat baking tin, sprinkle with a little cinnamon sugar, spread dabs of butter over the top, and bake for a short while with heat from above. Serve lukewarm. A few rosettes of whisked cream are an optional garnish.

HOT APPLE CAKES
ELDERFLOWER FRITTERS

APPLE CAKES
20 g (²/₃ oz) yeast
250 ml (9 fl oz) milk
150 g (5 oz) plain flour
4 apples
2 tablespoons sugar
1 pinch salt
grated rind of ½ an
untreated lemon
4 eggs
50 g (2 oz) sultanas
50 g (2 oz) chopped hazelnuts, butter for frying
2 tablespoons sugar
1 pinch cinnamon

ELDERFLOWER FRITTERS
12 elderflower clusters
100 g (4 oz) plain flour
140 ml (5 fl oz) milk
2 egg yolks
2 teaspoons sugar
grated rind of ½ an
untreated lemon
salt
2 egg whites
fat for frying, icing sugar
4 scoops of vanilla ice-
cream, whipping cream

HOT APPLE CAKES (below)
Dissolve the yeast in the luke-warm milk. Put the flour in a basin, make a well in the centre, and stir in the milk with the yeast. Add the peeled, cored, and diced apples together with the rest of the ingredients, and mix well. Cover with a cloth, and let the dough rise in a warm place for 20–30 minutes.
Then scoop out tablespoons of dough, and fry in a pan with butter. Dip the still hot cakes in cinnamon-sugar, and serve immediately.

ELDERFLOWER FRITTERS (above)
The flower clusters should be in full bloom. Wash them under running water, and drain on kitchen paper.
Sieve the flour, stir into the milk, and beat the egg yolks into the mixture with a whisk. Add the sugar, grated lemon rind, and a pinch of salt. Finally, beat the egg whites, and fold into the mixture. Allow the batter to rest for a while. Take the elderflowers by the stem, dip them in the batter, remove, let the excess batter drip off, then fry them in hot fat for 2–3 minutes. Dust with icing sugar, and serve with ice-cream and whipped cream.

The elder grows along the edges of woods and paths or against buildings. Its blossoms and fruit are now hardly used, but our grandmothers made good use of both. A generous dash of elder syrup in a glass of mineral water makes a refreshing summer drink. Elderberry jam, made with a third of tart apples, and possibly a touch of lemon and cinnamon, is a delicacy that is hardly available commercially. Elderberry wine, "champagne", and tea, were also favourites in the past. In our recipe it is the elderberry flowers that give the fritters their distinctive flavour.

RHUBARB FLAN
CHERRY TARTS

RHUBARB FLAN
The short pastry:
200 g (7 oz) self-raising flour
1 pinch salt
75 g (3 oz) sugar
grated rind of ½ untreated lemon
100 g (4 oz) margarine
1 egg or 2 egg yolks
1 tablespoon rum

The filling:
500 g (1 lb) rhubarb
5–6 egg whites
200 g (7 oz) icing sugar
125 g ground almonds

CHERRY TARTS
Short pastry of 150 g (5 oz) self-raising flour
800 g (1¾ lb) cherries
3 egg yolks
80 g (3 oz) sugar
3 rusk slices
250 g (9 oz) sour cream
3 egg whites

NB:
Currants can be used instead of rhubarb in the flan recipe. Margarine makes the pastry lighter than butter. The cherry tarts, served warm, make a pleasant change for tea. On hot days they can also be served with vanilla ice-cream as a dessert.

RHUBARB FLAN (below)
Sieve the flour into a basin, and mix with the salt, sugar, lemon rind, and the margarine cut into slivers. Form a well in the mixture, and add the egg and rum. Quickly knead into a smooth dough, and put in a cold place. Preheat the oven to 200 °C / 400 °F (fan assisted ovens to 160 °C / 325 °F).
Roll the dough out thin, line a flan ring, pressing the dough against the side of the tin, and prick the bottom of the flan case several times with a fork. For the filling, peel the rhubarb, and cut into short pieces; if you are using a fan-assisted oven, pre-cook the rhubarb briefly. Beat the egg whites, and stir in the sugar and almonds. Mix half of this with the rhubarb, and fill the flan case with the mixture. Spread the rest of the egg-white mixture over the top. Bake in the preheated oven for about 45 minutes (30–35 minutes in fan-assisted ovens). To prevent the top from becoming too brown, cover for a while with buttered greaseproof paper.

CHERRY TARTS (above)
Kirschküchle
Prepare the pastry as in the previous recipe, and put in a cold place. Preheat the oven to 160°C (325 °F). Stone the washed cherries.
Mix the egg yolk and sugar thoroughly, and add the grated rusks together with the sour cream. Roll out the pastry, and line cassolettes with it, pricking the pastry a few times with a fork. Fill the tart cases with the cherries. Beat the egg white till stiff, fold into the mixture, and cover the cherries with it.
Bake the tarts in the preheated oven until the tops are light brown (about 20 minutes).

Under "Rhubarb", a German cookery book published in 1893, says: ". . . it is seen in various forms as a decorative plant in gardens; and for the last 20–30 years, especially in England – and more recently also here in Germany – the thick stems have been increasingly used as a kind of fruit, stewed, as jam, and for various desserts, cakes, soups, etc, and also for a very popular home-made wine."

CHEESECAKE
RED WINE CAKE

CHEESECAKE
The short pastry:
180 g (6½ oz) self-raising flour
120 g (4½ oz) margarine
60 g (2 oz) sugar
2 egg yolks

The filling:
250 g (9 oz) cottage cheese
2 egg yolks
125 ml (4½ fl oz) milk
35 g (1½ oz) sultanas
10 g (⅓ oz) vanilla sugar
1½ tablespoons flour
2 egg whites
2 tablespoons sugar
dabs of butter

RED WINE CAKE
300 g (11 oz) butter
300 g (11 oz) sugar
125 ml (4½ fl oz) red wine
300 g (11 oz) self-raising flour
6 egg yolks
150 g (5 oz) grated chocolate
1½ teaspoons cinnamon
1½ teaspoons cocoa
10 g vanilla sugar
6 egg whites

CHEESECAKE (below)
Quickly knead a dough out of the pastry ingredients, and put in a cool place. Preheat the oven to 160 °C (325 °F). Pass the cottage cheese through a fine sieve. Add the egg yolks, milk, the roughly chopped sultanas, vanilla sugar, and flour. Roll out the dough thin, and line a buttered baking sheet with it, pricking the bottom a number of times with a fork. Beat the egg whites stiff, carefully fold into the cottage cheese mixture, and cover the pastry with it. Bake in the preheated oven for 30–35 minutes. Serve the cheesecake lukewarm (do not turn it out, but cut it into pieces on the baking sheet), and serve a scoop of ice-cream with each piece.

RED WINE CAKE (above)
Cream the butter and sugar. Stir in the red wine, then the flour and egg yolks, gradually adding the rest of the ingredients, except for the egg whites. Finally, fold in the stiffly beaten white of egg by the spoonful. Fill a loaf tin with the dough, put the tin in the cold oven; bake for 15 minutes at 200 °C (400 °F), and then for a further 1 hour 20 minutes at about 180°C (350 °F).

Cottage cheese is, of course, not really cheese; but it can be used to make cheese – and also to make this wonderful "cheesecake", as has been practised in Swabia through the ages. American and English recipes for similar cakes often call for cream cheese as a base.

PLUM TERRINE IN MARZIPAN

200 g (7 oz) fresh plums
50 g (2 oz) sugar
4 tablespoons port
2 tablespoons Armagnac
200 g (7 oz) prunes
30 g (1 oz) marzipan
2 tablespoons plum brandy
3 leaves gelatine
15 g (½ oz) walnuts
20 g (⅔ oz) shelled pistachio nuts
20 g (⅔ oz) pine kernels
1 orange in segments with
skin removed
15 g (½ oz) grated rind of
an untreated orange

The marzipan cover:
150 g (5 oz) marzipan
40 g (1½ oz) icing sugar

Stone the plums (they should be large and juicy), boil them up with the sugar, port, and Armagnac, then rub through a sieve. Quarter the prunes and boil up in the purée of plums. Mix the marzipan with the plum brandy.

Soak the gelatine leaves in cold water, squeeze the water out of them, and dissolve them in the warm plum purée. Combine the marzipan sauce with the purée, then stir in the walnuts, pista-chios, pine kernels, the orange segments, and the grated orange peel. Fill a loaf form with the mixture and refrigerate over-night.

Roll out the marzipan on icing sugar for the cover, and wrap it round the now cold terrine. Re-frigerate again before cutting.

This delicious dessert is a modern, more sophisticated equivalent of the traditional fruit bread that is made before Christ-mas in Swabia and other parts of Germany. Fruit bread is based mainly on dried local fruits – especially the pear – and spices, and is eaten either with or with-out butter.

ANISEED BISCUITS
SWABIAN DOUGHNUTS

ANISEED BISCUITS OR
COOKIES
4 eggs
500 g (generous 1 lb) icing
sugar
500 g (generous 1 lb) self-
raising flour
1 tablespoon rum
1 pinch salt
butter for the baking sheet
2 tablespoons aniseed for
sprinkling

SWABIAN DOUGHNUTS
Basic yeast dough recipe:
500 g (generous 1 lb) plain
flour
15 g (½ oz) yeast
50 g (2 oz) sugar
250 ml (9 fl oz) milk
1 teaspoon salt
1–2 eggs
50–75 g (2–3 oz) butter

750 g (1¾ lb) lard or
1 litre (1¾ pints) oil for
deep frying
cinnamon and sugar for
sprinkling

NB:
*Store the aniseed biscuits
in a tin together with
pieces of apple so that
they do not get too hard.
The yeast dough for the
Swabian doughnuts can be
used as a basis for a number of other kinds of fruit
cakes and doughnuts.*

ANISEED BISCUITS (below)
Beat the eggs and icing sugar for about 20 minutes, till frothy. Mix this with the flour, rum, and salt, and knead into a dough. Allow the dough to rest for 1–2 hours. Roll out the dough about 7mm (⅓ inch) thick on a surface dusted with flour. Press the floured moulds firmly on the dough, flouring the moulds afresh each time, until the whole area is covered. Sprinkle a little aniseed onto the buttered baking sheet. Cut out the individual biscuits from the dough, and place on the baking sheet with a knife. Cover with a cloth and allow to dry overnight.
On the following day preheat the oven to 150 °C (300 °F), and then bake the biscuits on the middle shelf for about 25 minutes until they have risen.
In order to keep them white on top, cover after 15 minutes with greaseproof paper.
Brush off any flour still on top of the biscuits and keep them covered with a cloth in a cool room for a few days, so that they lose their crispness.

SWABIAN DOUGHNUTS (above)
Sieve the flour into a basin, and put in a warm place. Dissolve the yeast with some sugar in luke-warm milk; pour this mixture into a well formed in the flour, and stir some of the surrounding flour into it. Dust with flour, and put the basin covered with a cloth in a warm place.
After about 30 minutes, when this first dough has risen well, stir in the sugar, salt, eggs, the melted butter, and the rest of the lukewarm milk, and knead and beat the mixture together with the remaining flour until it easily detaches from the spoon and the side of the basin. Put the finished dough in a warm place for about 1½ hours until it has risen.
Heat the frying fat in a pot. Roll out the dough to finger thickness, and cut into lozenge shapes. Allow to rise again, and then deep-fry. Sprinkle with cinnamon and sugar while still warm – and eat soon!

THE RECIPES
ACCORDING TO GROUPS

Unless otherwise stated, the amounts given are for four servings.

Photographs

Bavaria: 58 (M. u. H.), 60 (Hans Reinhard), 142 (Sauer)

Hans Joachim Döbbelin: 66

Bruno Hausch: 10

Erhard Hehl: 40/41, 42, 45 t., 45 b., 48/49

Huber: 176 (Jürgen Richter)

IFA-Bilderteam: 46 (Digul), 53 (Müller)

Foto-Ingeborg: 37 b.

Karlheinz Käppeler: 17, 22, 29 t., 31, 122, 158

Waltraud Klammet-Mochel: 34 t., 37 t.

Mauritius: 15 (Schwarz), 27 (Mehlig)

Friedhelm Messow: 6, 21, 23, 28, 36, 50, 102, 144

Thomas Pfündel: 33

Günther Schmidt: 2, 35, 47, 154, 164

Sigloch-Bildarchiv: 38/39 (Baumann); 29 b., 54/55, 62, 82/83, 86, 92/93, 114, 132/133, 166/167 and all the uneven page numbers from 57 to 186 (Döbbelin); 13, 18, 72 (Hehl); 7, 68 (van Hoorick); 90 (Marco Schneiders); 12, 34 b. (Toni Schneiders); 8, 11, 19, 25, 32, 38, 43, 51, 110 (Spiegelhalter)

Studio für Landkartentechnik Hamburg: 4/5

© SIGLOCH Edition, Am Buchberg 8, D-74572 Blaufelden
Internet: www.sigloch.de
Printed and bound by: A/S Preses Nams, Riga – Latvia
ISBN 978-389393-093-7

OUR CULINARY GEMS

REIS

NUDELN

KUCHEN & TORTEN

VORSPEISEN

AKTIV & VITAL

NIEDERSACHSEN
Kulinarische Streifzüge

SCHWABEN
Kulinarische Streifzüge

SCHLESWIG-HOLSTEIN
Kulinarische Streifzüge

BAYERN
Kulinarische Streifzüge

MECKLENBURG
Kulinarische Streifzüge

SACHSEN
Kulinarische Streifzüge

THÜRINGEN
Kulinarische Streifzüge

BADEN
Kulinarische Streifzüge

BERLIN
BRANDENBURG
Kulinarische Streifzüge

ODENWALD
Kulinarische Streifzüge

SCHWEIZ
Kulinarische Streifzüge

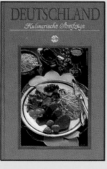

DEUTSCHLAND
Kulinarische Streifzüge

ÖSTERREICH
Kulinarische Streifzüge

EUROPA
Kulinarische Streifzüge

FRANKREICH
Kulinarische Streifzüge